What Homebuyers Should Know about Buying a Home

WHAT HOMEBUYERS SHOULD KNOW ABOUT BUYING A HOME

Albert H. Knox

VANTAGE PRESS
New York / Washington / Atlanta
Los Angeles / Chicago

FIRST EDITION

Copyright © 1987 by Albert H. Knox

Published by Vantage Press, Inc.
516 West 34th Street, New York, New York 10001

Manufactured in the United States of America
ISBN: 0-533-06883-5

Library of Congress Catalog Card No.: 85-91377

Contents

Preface

Purchasing a home is almost invariably the most expensive transaction that a person will ever make. There are many ways of financing a home. Most homebuyers are not familiar with these various financial concepts. Because of their lack of knowledge of the principles and financial practices of real estate, many buyers find themselves in homes that they cannot afford. They eventually lose the homes through foreclosure. Their credit is seriously damaged, which affects future financial transactions.

The purpose of this book is to make homebuyers aware of the methods, procedures, and implications of purchasing and owning a home. This book is designed for the buyers and sellers of homes; however, it can serve as a manual for real estate brokers, sales agents, and investors.

This book covers many important factors relating to real estate. It brings together information that virtually every person negotiating a real estate transaction can use to prevent or eliminate potential problems. This book is not designed to eliminate the need for the services and/or legal advice of a real estate attorney. It will assist those persons contemplating buying real estate to understand the real estate market. This book also contains many mathematical models that explain complicated real estate computations. Abstract real estate concepts are translated to simple mathematical formulas, which will help buyers and sellers to understand lenders' underwriting standards.

What Homebuyers Should Know about Buying a Home

How to Select a Real Estate Broker

Chosing the wrong real estate broker can create nightmares for home-buyers. It is therefore imperative for homebuyers to select a competent and honest real estate broker. The most important thing for the home-buyer to keep in mind is the fact that the broker represents the seller and not the buyer. Too often, the buyers have the impression that the broker is their representative. This impression could render the buyers vulnerable to the favoritism that the broker will invariably have for the seller, whom he represents as the principal agent. Loyalty will primarily be given to the seller, and in the negotiation proceedings, the broker in most cases will support the seller's position.

There are some unscrupulous real estate brokers who use a variety of clandestine actions to induce unsuspecting buyers to purchase un-affordable homes or homes with defects that have been deliberately concealed. The homebuyer should develop a system to identify these brokers. There are several things that homebuyers can do to detect an unscrupulous and incompetent broker. A buyer can get a reliable report on the honesty and integrity of a real estate broker by asking buyers who have purchased homes listed by the broker. The brokers' previous customers are often quite willing to discuss the problems or satisfaction that they have experienced with particular real estate brokers. If the broker is unwilling to reveal the identity of previous customers, he may be concealing the identity to keep damaging information from surfacing. The homebuyer should be suspicious of real estate brokers who use the privacy or confidentiality of customers as a reason for not revealing their identities. The homebuyer can obtain information about the broker by locating buyers who have purchased homes listed by the broker. This can be done by driving around in the neighborhoods where the brokers have real estate signs that list the homes as "SOLD." By contacting the sellers and making them aware of the purpose for knowing the buyer's identity, the homebuyer can obtain much valuable information concerning the broker's character, integrity, honesty, and competency. This information can be used to assist the buyers in mak-ing a decision to select a particular real estate broker.

Other measures that the homebuyer can take to find information about the real estate broker are contacting the state real estate commission and the Better Business Bureau. These two organizations receive complaints from consumers and homebuyers concerning the practices and actions of real estate firms. By contacting them, the homebuyer can obtain information about the frequency of complaints that have been filed against the brokers. Real estate brokers who have had numerous complaints filed against them should be avoided by homebuyers or a competent real estate attorney should be obtained to conduct the real estate transactions in order to ascertain that the language used in the contract will not create any potential legal complications. The most reliable information, of course, will be the testimony of the brokers' previous customers.

Buying a home generally requires several months of searching for the right home in the right neighborhood and for an appropriate price. This time can be utilized by the buyer to monitor the sales activity of a real estate broker. If homes are sold on a frequency basis, the implications could denote that the buyers and sellers are satisfied with the way the real estate brokers negotiate and consummate sales transactions. In any event, sales activity will give the buyer more leads to investigate; hence a more reliable profile of the broker can be obtained. Real estate brokers who provide frequent training for their sales staff will generally have a competent and well-trained sales staff who have a high level of professionalism. This type of information can be discovered by checking the help wanted section of the newspaper. Many reputable real estate firms will emphasize that continuous training is available for their sales staff. This practice by real estate firms generally attracts competent, dedicated salespersons with a high degree of integriity and unmitigated honesty. These real estate firms should be checked and contacted. They often provide real estate services and information that less innovative and reputable firms are not willing to provide.

Many real estate brokers are members of the National Association of Realtors. This is a close-knit organization comprised of real estate brokers whose objective is to promote a high level of professionalism and impeccable integrity among its members. Real estate brokers who have a reputation of conducting nebulous real estate transactions and who have many complaints filed against them for negotiating shoddy and inferior real estate transactions are not permitted to become members.

The homebuyers may contact the state's branch of the National Association of Realtors to obtain a list of members who are in good standing with the organization. From this list, the homebuyer can choose several real estate brokers who meet the selective criteria that have been discussed in this section. It is of paramount importance for the buyers to procure the services of a real estate attorney to review the contract in order to prevent ambiguities in the real estate phraseology that may result in litigation. To obtain addition protection, the homebuyer can obtain a bonded housing inspector to conduct an intensive inspection of the home's major systems, such as electrical, plumbing, and structural. Any defects detected can be compromised and compensated for by incorporating specific terms and conditions in the contract. A real estate broker can mean the difference between the successful consummation and cancellation of a real estate sales transaction; therefore, the buyers should certainly be cognizant of safety measures that can be taken to alleviate or eliminate complications. The buyers would be wise to use the adage "An ounce of prevention is worth a pound of cure" in selecting a real estate broker. The efforts made by the homebuyers to investigate the broker's honesty, integrity, and competency are invaluable when compared to the costs that may evolve from mistakes or deliberate actions designed by the broker to mislead the homebuyer into buying a home requiring extensive repairs. By using selective criteria to choose a real estate broker, the homebuyer can reduce the chance of being involved in a costly real estate transaction consummated by an unscrupulous broker.

Neighborhood Selection

Selecting a neighborhood in which to purchase a home is invariably one of the most important aspects of the home buying process. The buyers will live in the neighborhood for many years, so it is extremely important to make the right choice. What may appear to be a bargain could turn into a sad and costly mistake. Many buyers have purchased homes without conducting an evaluation of the neighborhoods in which they will reside. One of the first steps in selecting a neighborhood is to determine how much one can afford to pay for housing. A very good policy is not to allow the total housing expense to exceed 30 percent of the gross income. The cost of housing and the homebuyers' income will determine the number of options of neighborhoods where home-buyers can afford to purchase homes. If the guidelines show that the maximum mortgage amount that the homebuyers can afford is $75,500, the homebuyers would be wasting their time looking in neighborhoods containing homes costing $85,500 and above, unless the buyers have the financial capacity to pay a substantial amount down in order to reduce the mortgage amount to an affordable level. Regardless of how much the homebuyers like the neighborhood or the number of attractive amenities the neighborhood has, the homebuyers should not allow themselves to be talked into buying a home that they cannot afford.

The location of the neighborhood should be one of the key factors considered when making a decision to purchase a home. The home should be located in neighborhoods where the homes are highly marketable. If some unfortunate condition or event such as unemployment, relocation or a divorce, occurs, that forces the homeowners to sell, they could put their home on the market and sell it without suffering a financial loss. The resale potential should be strong; many homeowners have lost virtually all of the equity that had been accumulated in their home because of a poor choice of location. Buyers should avoid purchasing homes in neighborhoods where the rate of resale is extremely low. Information concerning the marketability of homes located in selected neighborhoods can be obtained from real estate agents who have homes listed for sale and from residents living in the neighborhoods. Neighborhood appearance is another significant aspect of the home selection process. The appearance of other homes in the area can have a detrimental affect on property values. Buyers should avoid buying in neighborhoods that contain homes that are deteriorating and poorly maintained. The buyers should check the neighborhoods for conditions such as poorly landscaped yards, abandoned cars, and other rubbish and junk. The appearance of the neighborhoods can also adversely affect property values and eventually the potential resale of the property.

The quality of schools is also a desirable element that should be considered in selecting a neighborhood. It would be to the advantage of homebuyers to visit schools in the neighborhoods to get an idea of the educational programs and to observe the complete educational environment. Many homebuyers have purchased homes in areas where the schools' educational environment does not provide a positive and proper setting for students to learn. One excellent source of information concerning the quality of education can be obtained from talking to neighborhood residents. The marketability of homes is affected by the quality of the schools. Neighborhoods containing good-quality schools have a low homeowner turnover rate. Homes are sold on a frequent basis in these neighborhoods when they are listed for sale. They do not remain on the market long, because of the high demand for them.

Many buyers have purchased homes in neighborhoods because of other desired amenties or because of special attractions of the home. Because of the type and conditions of the school, they enroll their children in private schools or send them to another school in another neighborhood. The importance of good-quality schools cannot be overemphasized. It could be the determining factor in some sales transactions.

The choice of neighborhoods should also be selected in accordance with the homebuyers' living style. If the buyers enjoy participating in recreational activities, they should select a neighborhood that has access to various kinds of recreation, such as parks with tennis facilities, jogging paths, golfing, and other sports activities. The home may have all the desired amenities that the homebuyers want, but the neighborhood may not have other features that coincide with the homebuyers' living styles. The enjoyment of owning a home could be affected by the lack of certain amenities or the existence of certain conditions. For example, the Collins family purchased a home in a neighborhood because the home had a lovely landscaped yard and a large swimming pool in the backyard. The Collins family consisted of high-school teenage students, one child that attended elementary school, and one preschool child. Both Mr. and Mrs Collins worked. The neighborhood did not have access to daycare facilities for preschool children. The closest major shopping facilities were located in another neighborhood that had a traffic problem. The closest park was located two miles from the home. By analyzing the facts and neighborhood conditions, we see that the Collins family purchased a home in the wrong neighborhood. First, the home's resale potential is poor. If the Collins had to move because of circumstances beyond their control, it would probably take them a long time to sell the home. They might have to make special concessions because of the neighborhood. There were no daycare facilities for pre-school children; therefore, the Collins will have to locate a daycare facility in another neighborhood.

Homebuyers should make a complete assessment of their housing needs. They should also visit the neighborhoods where they plan to buy homes to observe the conditions and make notes of neighborhood amenties and undesirable elements. Homebuyers should not be influenced by frills and housing cosmetics such as fancy wallpaper, expensive carpeting or decorative light fixtures. These items cannot adequately replace the convenience and the enjoyment that the homebuyer would receive from other essential neighborhood amenities.

Negotiating the Purchase Price

Businesses use the free enterprise system in marketing products and services. The law of supply and demand has a pronounced impact on the sales price of products and services. Generally, all other things being equal, a large supply causes a decrease in demand. When the Florida orange growers produce bumper crops, the price of orange juice decreases as demand decreases. When builders overbuild, the prices of homes have a natural propensity for decreasing. The same effect occurs when there is a glut of existing homes on the market for sale. However, this demand-supply effect is often overlooked by homebuyers. Oftentimes sellers and buyers are motivated by personal preferences and special conditions that affect the sales prices of homes.

The buyer should become familiar with negotiating techniques before attempting to purchase a home. There are many cases where overzealous buyers were easily talked into buying a home that was not suited for their needs or when the financing plan was not compatible with their financial capacities. Over- or underbuying has caused many financial problems for homebuyers. Not until the real estate transaction was closed and the buyers occupied the homes did they realize the costly mistake that was made in buying a particular home. Homebuyers should make an assessment of the reasons why a seller wants to sell. Prices are often established and contingent upon the seller's particular circumstances. Generally, there are three kinds of sellers. Each type of seller is motivated to sell their homes because of varying and compelling conditions. The three types of sellers are: (1) the envisionary seller, (2) the opportunist seller, and (3) the distressed seller. Identifying the type of seller will give the buyer an opportunity to take advantages of specific circumstances to successfully negotiate a beneficial sales price.

The envisionary seller is one who thinks he wants to sell so that he can purchase the home of his dream or accomplish some other desired task. These are often sellers who are difficult to negotiate with because they want a more elegant home but cannot seem to bring their wants and desires into the proper perspective. Many times, after they have compared the cost of the new envisionary elegant home or other desired task with their present situation or home, they establish a high selling price and become extremely adamant in not negotiating a compromise on the sales price. Very often these envisionary sellers are suffering from temporary housing or situational euphoria and subconsciously put their house on the market to see what price it will eventually bring. These are perhaps the most difficult sellers with whom to negotiate a sales price. They are generally not extremely serious or anxious about selling their homes. They are affected by emotions and envisionary possibilities that become unrealistic visions.

The buyer should not allow special features of the home to influence his decision. The sales price should always be at or below the market value of the home. An overzealous buyer may be talked into purchasing a home from an enthusiastic envisionary seller by an agressive and assertive salesperson The buyer is inadverently induced to purchase a home by the salesperson capitalizing on the buyer's high interest level and the special appeal of specific amenties such as curtains, floor tile, wall decoration, or other things that contribute little or nothing to either the value or functional utility of the home. Although certain amenties do increase the value of a home, these amenities alone should not be the factors that determine the sales price or influence the buyer to purchase. Knowing the reason for the sale of the property will enable the buyer to take a more realistic and objective negotiating approach. The envisionary seller often creates unnecessary problems that cause delays in consummating the transaction. Very often, he wants the buyer to make concessions to his advantage. He is unyielding, because he feels that he has to maximize his profit from the sale to compensate for the additional cost of pursuing his more elegant home or procuring some desired visionary project. The buyer should avoid the envisionary seller, if possible, unless he is prepared to spend an exorbitant amount of time negotiating and not be disappointed for making concessions that he might not have been prepared to make. Envisionary sellers will sometimes make unrealistic demands, subconsciously hoping that the buyer will reject them. This gives the seller an opportunity to curtail the negotiations to seek a more willing and suceptible buyer.

The distressed seller is perhaps the most vulnerable seller. He is motivated to sell because of involuntary conditions and circumstances. These sellers are generally indifferent, caring very little about the sales price or other concessions. The element of time may have adverse effects on distressed sellers. They usually want to or have to sell within a certain period of time. Maximizing profits on the sale of their homes has virtually no significance to them. They are mostly concerned about how soon a sale can be consummated. The typical distressed seller is a person who has recently reached a divorce settlement in which the court has ordered the property to be sold. The most difficult obstacle is getting the co-mortgagors, man and wife, to agree on a sales price. The buyer will frequently encounter situations where the co-mortgagors, because of the divorce, are hostile toward each other. It then becomes extremely difficult to establish a sales price. One co-mortgagor becomes belligerent and uncooperative because of the other co-mortgagor's decision. Should this situation occur, it becomes necessary to negotiate with both co-mortgagors at the same time or with the co-mortgagors' attorneys.

Another illustration of the distressed seller is a person who loses his job and cannot afford to make the mortgage payments on the home. The seller may be faced with imminent foreclosure and want to sell the home before the lender forecloses, to prevent losing the equity that has been accumulated in the home and to protect his credit rating.

Having knowledge of the conditions and motives that are motivating a person to sell a home will give the buyer an advantage to negotiate terms and concessions that are favorable. It could also be used to expedite the sales negotiations and reduce the time needed to consummate the transactions.

Identifying the distressed seller is an easier task than identifying the envisionary or opportunist seller. Very often the envisionary seller will react like an opportunist seller. The distressed seller can always be identified by noting the following: (1) The distressed seller will invariably assume an indifferent attitude. The salesperson will do virtually all of the negotiating. The buyer must realize that the salesperson is acting on behalf of the seller. The size of his commission is contingent upon the sale and the price of the home. However, if time is a factor, such as in impending foreclosure, the buyer would be in an excellent bargaining position.

The opportunist seller is motivated to sell his home because of a compelling desire to capitalize on an opportunity that occurs at infrequent intervals. An example would be where a homeowner has an opportunity of starting a business or purchasing a larger home at a price below its fair market value, but does not have the financial capacity to take advantage of the opportunity. The opportunist sellers are easier to negotiate a compromise with because they have virtually an insatiable desire to achieve their objectives. It is imperative that the buyers be aware of the sellers' motives so that their negotiating strategies can induce the sellers into a compromised sales agreement.

9

Unlike the envisionary seller, the opportunist seller is more willing to make compromises and agree to terms and conditions that are favorable to the buyer. The opportunist seller can easily be identified through the following actions: (1) frequent contacts with the salesperson or the buyer, (2) concerns about the buyer's credit and income capacity, (3) eagerness to correct deficiences that were uncovered by an inspection of the home, and (4) concerns about the amount of the earnest money and when it will be submitted by the buyer. These actions by the seller should give the buyer the negotiating edge in establishing a sales price. The fact that should be of paramount importance to the buyer is that, generally, the opportunist seller is under no great financial pressure to sell his home. He has the financial means to retain his home if so desired. The most compelling factor for selling is the strong desire to take advantage of an opportunity to sell his home at an opportune time for a fair price that will enable him to realize his objective.

Another example of an opportunist seller is a homeowner approaching retirement age who plans to purchase a smaller home or move into housing complex for senior citizens. The seller usually is not pressured with the time factor; therefore, the buyer should use a less aggressive diplomatic approach in negotiating the sales price. It is therefore important for the buyer to use an approach that would focus on the seller's needs rather than displaying an overzealous interest in purchasing the home.

Buyers should always make a thorough analysis of the motives behind the sale and become familiar with the neighborhood conditions and amenities. This will greatly enhance their negotiation powers.

4

Finding Out How Much
You Can Afford for Housing

Most homebuyers are not aware of how much they can afford to spend for housing or what size mortgage they can qualify for within their financial capacity. Lenders have established debt-income and housing expense ratios that homebuyers should not exceed. These are part of the home loan underwriting standards that the homebuyers must meet to purchase a home. Most conventional loans require that the home-buyers' total housing expense not exceed 25 to 28 percent of their gross monthly income. Other recurring bills that take ten months or more to pay off may not exceed 36 percent of the gross income. Due to individual circumstances, these standards may be modified by the lenders.

The following illustration is used to explain how a homebuyer can determine the income needed to qualify for a specific mortgage amount. The payment on a thirty-year conventional mortgage of $65,000 at 14 percent interest is $770. Assume that the property tax is forty dollars, hazard insurance twenty-five dollars, and mortgage insurance twenty dollars per month. The total housing expense would be $855. The amount of income needed to qualify for the mortgage is $2,850 ($855 housing expense divided by 30 percent housing expense ratio). The ratio used by the lender depends on individual circumstances. Credit deficiencies may cause the lender to use a lower housing expense ratio or even reject the loan application. With the introduction of innovative home financing plans, the initial mortgage payments during the first few years may be reduced to enable the homebuyer to meet the housing and debt-income ratios with less income. The higher the housing expense ratio the lender allows the homebuyer to have, the less income is needed to qualify. For example, in the previous illustration, if the lender establishes a 35 percent housing expense ratio, the homebuyer would need only $2,443 monthly income to qualify for the mortgage ($855 housing expense divided by thirty five percent housing expense ratio). The homebuyer would need even less income if he uses an interest buy-down plan for financing the home. If the builder uses a 3 percent buy-down plan, the interest rate will be 11 percent (14 percent prevailing market rate less 3 percent buy-down). The mortgage payment would be $619, principal and interest. By adding the other housing expenses, forty dollars for the property tax, twenty-five dollars for hazard insurance, and twenty dollars for mortgage insurance, the total housing expense would be $704. Dividing the total housing expense by 30 percent, the homebuyer would need only $2,347 monthly gross income to qualify, compared to the $2,850 needed without the 3 percent buy-down plan. High housing expense ratios, however, may impose a financial burden on the homebuyers if they lack financial management skills such as budgeting and fail to use debt control measures to avoid excessive financial obligations. The lack of the ability to use financial control measures could result in the homebuyer defaulting on the mortgage, causing the lender to foreclose on the home.

HOW TO CALCULATE THE MORTGAGE AMOUNT

To find out what amount of a mortgage a homebuyer can afford, several computations are necessary, Assume a homebuyer with a combined gross annual income of $36,500 per year. Dividing by 12, the monthly gross income can be computed ($36,500 divided by 12) as $3,042. If the lender uses a housing expense ratio of 30 percent of gross income, the homebuyer total monthly housing expense could not exceed $912. This amount must include hazard insurance, property tax, and mortgage insurance. If the housing expenses are: $40 for the property tax, $20 for hazard insurance, and $20 for mortgage insurance, the total amount that the homebuyer could afford to apply toward the mortgage would be $832 (The total amount the homebuyer can afford is $912, less $80 housing expenses.) This figure is used to determine the maximum mortgage amount that the homebuyer can afford. By checking the 14 percent interest rate table for a thirty-year loan in the appendix, we see the maximum mortgage that the homebuyer could afford is $70,000. Since the total housing expense is used to determine how much a homebuyer can afford, it is necessary to know the amount of the property taxes, hazard insurance, and mortgage insurance before the mortgage amount can be determined. The mortgage amount that the homebuyer can qualify for is affected and determined by the interest rate. The lower the interest rate, the higher the amount of mortgage the homebuyer can afford. The total debt income ratio is generally the ratio that prevents homebuyers from qualifying to purchase a home. The debt-income ratio is comprised of the total housing expense plus recurring bills that require more than ten months to pay off. To use an example, suppose Hudson is attempting to purchase a home that costs $65,500. He pays $5,000 as a down payment, which leaves a $60,500 mortgage. The mortgage payment on a thirty-year 14 percent $60,500 mortgage is $716. Other monthly housing expenses include $35 for property taxes and $25 for hazard insurance. The total housing expense is $776. If the lender uses a 40 percent debt-income ratio and Hudson's gross monthly income is $3,575, his monthly debts could not exceed $1,430 ($3,575 gross monthly income × 40 percent, lender's debt-income ratio). Assume that Hudson's debts include the following: $450 for two auto loans, $150 for three charge accounts, and $135 for two installment accounts. The total monthly recurring debt is $1,511. Since Hudson's total debts of $1,511 exceed the $1,430 maximum amount allowed by the lender's 40 percent debt-income ratio, his application for a home loan would probably be rejected. Hudson could reduce his debt-income ratio by paying off some of his debts. He would then meet the lender's home loan debt-income criteria. The income-required formula shows monthly incomes required to qualify for a home loan at various interest rates. The amounts are based upon a $65,000 mortgage for thirty years. The lender required housing expense ratio is 30 percent. The higher the interest, the more income is needed by the homebuyers to meet the lender's housing expense ratios. Some homebuyers are able to qualify for homes even though their debt-income ratios exceed the lenders' required standards. This occurs when the homebuyers have established a history of credit reliability. Their credit records are excellent, and they have shown that they have financial and budgetary skills to effectively manage their debts and incomes.

INCOME REQUIRED FORMULA

By using the total housing expense from the housing expense schedule described in this chapter, the amount of income needed to qualify for a thirty-year, 12 percent, $65,000 mortgage can be computed. In the following illustration, assume that the lender requires that the homebuyer's housing expense does not exceed 28 percent of the monthly gross income. The total housing expense and the lender's housing expense ratio are substituted into the formula to find the income needed to qualify for the mortgage.

INCOME REQUIRED = TOTAL HOUSING EXPENSE/
LENDER'S HOUSING EXPENSE RATIO

$$I = \frac{T\ H\ E}{L\ H\ E} \qquad\qquad I = \frac{\$714}{.28}$$

$$I = \$2,550$$

13

The amount of income required to qualify for any mortgage amount can be computed by using the above formula. It is, however, imperative that the total housing expenses be known, including property taxes, hazard insurance, and mortgage insurance. In addition, the lender's housing expense ratio must also be known before the amount of income can be computed.

INCOME REQUIRED AT VARIOUS INTEREST RATES

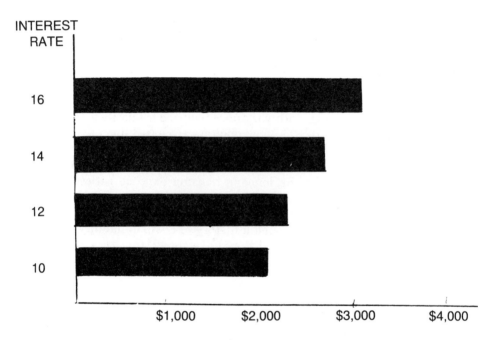

Income needed to qualify for a $65,000 mortgage at various interest rates. The lender requires that homebuyers pay no more than 30 percent of their gross income for housing expense.

HOUSING EXPENSE

	10%	12%	14%	16%
Principal and Interest	$570	$669	$770	$874
Property Taxes	30	30	30	30
Hazard Insurance	15	15	15	15
Total Housing Expense	$615	$714	$815	$919

To compute the amount of income needed to qualify for a specified mortgage amount, divide the total housing expense by the lender's established housing expense ratio. In the above illustration, if the interest rate were 14 percent, the total housing expense on a $65,000 mortgage would be $835. The following computation can be used to find the income needed by the homebuyer to qualify for a specific mortgage amount.

INCOME REQUIRED FORMULA

$$\text{Income Required} = \frac{\text{Total Housing Expense}}{\text{Lender's Housing Expense Ratio}}$$

CONVENTIONAL MORTGAGE FINANCING PRE-QUALIFY TEST

Conventional mortgages require the homebuyers to meet certain loan standards. The following standards are guidelines that are used to determine if the homebuyers have the financial capacity to meet the mortgage obligations of a specified mortgage amount. Homebuyers are also evaluated upon their respective credit profiles to see if they meet the credit standards. Serious credit deficiencies may prevent them from qualifying for a home loan.

CONVENTIONAL MORTGAGE STANDARDS

GROSS INCOME
COMBINED INCOME
Other Income
Total Income

HOUSING EXPENSE RATIO
Gross Income
Multiply by Test Ratio
Maximum Housing Expense
  Allowed

Homebuyer's housing expenses should not exceed housing expense test ratio amount.
Homebuyer's total monthly expense should not exceed total recurring expense test amount.

PROJECTED HOUSING
  EXPENSE
Principal and Interest
Property Taxes
Hazard Insurance
Mortgage Insurance
Total Housing Expense

TOTAL RECURRING MONTHLY
EXPENSE
Total Housing Expense
Child Support
Alimony
Child Care
Monthly Bills
    (Exceeding 10 months)
Social Security
Total Monthly Expense

MONTHLY EXPENSE RATIO
Gross Income
Multiply by Test Ratio
Maximum Total Monthly
Expense Allowed

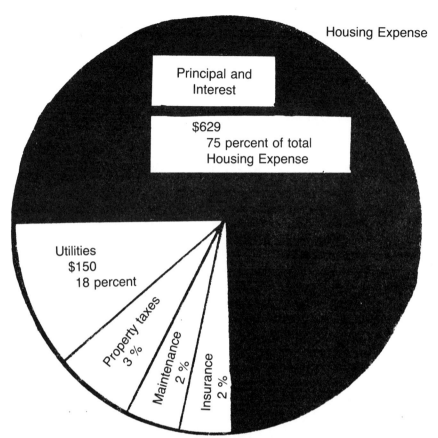

Housing Expense

Principal and Interest

$629
75 percent of total Housing Expense

Utilities
$150
18 percent

Property taxes
3%

Maintenance
2%

Insurance
2%

PERCENT OF TOTAL HOUSING EXPENSES

HOUSING EXPENSES	AMOUNT	PERCENT
Principal and Interest	$629	75%
Property Taxes	$ 25	3%
Home Maintenance	$ 20	2%
Hazard Insurance	$ 15	2%
Utilities	$150	18%
Totals	$839	100%

NOTE: The housing expenses were based upon estimates and a $55,500 thirty-year, 13½ percent mortgage.

5

Neighborhood Characteristics That May Affect Marketability of Homes

The market value of a home is invariably affected by neighborhood characteristics. Therefore, it is of paramount importance for the home-buyers to make a complete and accurate assessment of the neighborhood before the purchase agreement to buy a home is signed. Many homebuyers have purchased homes because of certain attractive features. The neighborhoods where the homes are located were not given much consideration. These homebuyers later found that the neighborhoods' environments were incompatible with their life-styles. In most cases, it is to the advantage of the homebuyers to purchase homes with fewer attractive features in neighborhoods with many desirable amenities and where the homes are highly marketable.

Homes located near congested traffic areas such as expressways may be affected by noise and traffic problems that spill over into adjacent neighborhoods. The traffic conditions could cause some of the vehicles to be diverted to neighborhoods, imposing hazardous traffic problems for the residents, especially small children. Homes that are located near airport traffic patterns may be confronted with annoying noise problems. This may also affect the resale of the homes. Many cities are now prohibiting the construction of housing within specified distances of airport runways. Airlines are also purchasing planes with quieter engines to reduce the noise level. Homes that are located near airports, where the noise level is readily apparent, generally remain on the market longer than homes that are not exposed to obnoxious noise problems.

UNDESIRABLE NEIGHBORHOOD ELEMENTS THAT CAUSE DECLINING PROPERTY VALUES

The two most important undesirable elements that affect market values and resale of homes are increasing crime, vandalism, and poorly maintained homes in the neighborhood. The crime factor is an intangible element that is not readily apparent, but once known by homebuyers becomes a virtually immovable sales barrier that prevents the homes from being sold. Not only are the homes difficult to sell, property values also decrease. Interviews with several homeowners who resided in neighborhoods that had high crime rates, including vandalism, disclosed that their homes had been on the market for sale for almost two years. The homeowners stated that they had to make many concessions and substantially lower the prices of their homes in order to negotiate sales agreements.

It is almost impossible to determine the level of crime in a particular neighborhood just by driving through it. One strong indicator that a neighborhood has a crime and vandalism problem is the number of homes that have window guards. Three or four homes on a block with window guards may be strong evidence that the neighborhood has an unusual high level of crime, including vandalism. The homebuyers should approach residents of the neighborhoods, especially those homeowners that have window guards installed, to inquire about the incidence of crime in the neighborhood. Homebuyers could also check with the police department for information concerning the types and frequency of crime in a particular neighborhood.

Home market values are also adversely affected by the condition and appearence of other homes in the neighborhoods. Poorly maintained homes cause property values to decrease. Neighborhoods that contain numerous deteriorating homes are responsible for extremely low resale rate of homes. Declining neighborhoods are readily apparent. They are characterized by excessive litter and rubbish on vacant lots, poorly maintained yards, homes with peeling and fading paint, abandoned vehicles, and nonconforming uses, such as various types of businesses' being operated from the homes in the neighborhoods. These conditions can be eliminated. However, the entire neighborhood must cooperate to form a homeowners' association to maximize the impact of various corrective measures that could be designed and initiated to improve the neighborhoods.

Most cities have developed neighborhood stabilization programs to control and remove conditions that cause neighborhood decay and deterioration. Homebuyers should be concerned about buying homes in older neighborhoods where neighborhood pride is lacking and signs of neighborhood decay are apparent.

The quality and availability of shopping facilities have a positive effect on the market values of homes. A complete range of stores specializing in a variety of consumer goods and services should be within reasonable traveling distance of a neighborhood. Many suburban neighborhoods have stylish homes with practically every conceivable modern convenience, but do not have immediate access to amenities that make a neighborhood pleasant and comfortable. Residents have to travel long distances for certain services. Most of these neighborhoods are relatively new and have not developed enough to support major shopping facilities. Therefore, residents are exposed to many inconveniences.

The location and the quality of educational facilities are two essential factors that make a neighborhood attractive and increase the market values of homes. Schools with inferior educational facilities located in areas that contain business operations turn away many prospective homebuyers. Consequently, the rate of resale of homes in the neighborhoods is very low. The quality of schools is one of the first factors that homebuyers with school-age children should consider when selecting a neighborhood to buy a home. One of the critical mistakes a family can make is purchasing a home in a neighborhood where the educational environment and facilities are inadequate and of poor quality. It is very important that the neighborhood has progressive and modern schools that offer recreational as well as educational programs for adults as well as children.

Neighborhood characteristics that homebuyers are most concerned about are those that are obvious and flagrant, such as dilapidated homes. Intangible characteristics are also important and may create many problems for homebuyers if they are not considered when selecting a neighborhood to buy a home.

Two of the most devastating conditions that can suppress market values of homes are: (a) poorly maintained homes and (b) factors that contribute to neighborhood decay. The marketability of homes can invariably be improved by correcting or removing negative elements that contribute to blight and neighborhood deterioration. The pictures below show housing in a neighborhood with depressed market values.

Neighborhood characteristics can adversely affect market values of homes.

Homes that are poorly maintained affect the value of other homes in the neighborhood. They also attract homebuyers who allow junk and debris to accumulate in their yards.

Homes that are in an advanced state of dilapidation, discourage homebuyers who take pride in maintaining their home.

6

Ways of Receiving Title and Owning Property

Most homebuyers purchase property without thinking about how the property will be distributed upon their death. This is the reason why a real estate professional or an attorney specializing in real estate should be consulted to interpret the effects of the various ways of receiving title to property. Probate courts generally are overloaded with cases where deceased property owners did not specify how the property was to be distributed upon their deaths. All homebuyers should consider what they want to happen to their property after their death. Failure to specify how property is to be distributed and apportioned has resulted in costly probate legal proceedings, where in many cases the attorneys representing the claimants or descendants of the deceased property owner will end up getting a larger percentage of the proceeds derived from the sale of the property than each of the claimants. The problem is complicated when a married couple having children from previous marriages fail to consider the legal ramifications that occur when benficiaries are not specified. The most common ways in which two or more persons own and receive title to property, especially husband and wife and the spouses in common-law marriages, are tenancy in common, joint tenancy, and tenancy by the entirety. The average homebuyer does not understand the effects of these different ways of owning property. In fact, many real estate agents are so concerned about earning a lucrative commission that they fail to interpret the effects of these different co-ownerships. The sales agents represent the seller; therefore, his interest is of primary concern. In a tenancy-in-common form of ownership, two or more persons may own property without having equal shares. If A, B, and C purchased property together, A could have a 50 percent share while B and C each own 25 percent. Each of the three co-owners has individual ownership in the property. Each can sell his share or encumber it with a creditor. The co-owners' property in joint ownership is subjected to the same credit proceedings as that of an individual property owner. This means that a judgement or lien can be placed on the co-owners' share for the

22

indebtedness. If Collins, Bates, and Dennis purchased a home together and Bates decided that he wanted to sell his share to Kale, neither Collins nor Dennis could prevent the sale to Kale. Should Dennis be killed in some kind of accident, his share would pass to his heirs and not to Kale and/or Bates. Another illustration that delineates the complications that could result from a tenancy in common co-ownership is where an unmarried couple, George and Mary, purchase a home together as a tenancy-in-common. Mary becomes extremely angry with George for dating another woman and decides that she no longer wanted to be a co-owner with George. Since Mary does not need George's approval, she could sell her share of the property to a third party, who could be one of Mary's relatives or perhaps even a boyfriend. This could result in a situation where either co-owner could petition the court to have the property sold, with each receiving his/her proportionate share from the proceeds of the sale of the property.

The homebuyers must be aware of the effects of the various ways of receiving title to property. They can then discuss their plans of having the property distributed after their death. The title to the property can be prepared in accordance to the homebuyers' intentions. Assume that Bill and Dolores purchased a home but wanted their children from a previous marriage to receive their share of the equity after their death. They purchased the home and received title as tenants in common. If Bill dies, Dolores would not receive his share of the equity; it would pass to his children. Suppose Bill has a grown daughter who does not get along with Dolores. The daughter could petition the court to have the property sold. If Dolores wanted to retain the home, she would have to buy the daughter's equity. The expense of buying the heirs' equity could be eliminated by carrying enough insurance on the co-owner to cover the cost.

Joint tenancy is used by many homebuyers. It can be created by clearly expressing the type of co-ownership desired by the buyers. Under joint tenancy, each co-owner has equal shares in the property. A co-owner in a joint tenancy ownership can convey his share to another person. This, in effect, would destroy the joint tenancy and change the ownership to a tenancy in common.

One of the most important characteristics of this kind of ownership is the right of survivorship. If Bob and Judy, unmarried, purchase a home and received title as joint tenants and not as community property, with rights of survivorship upon the death of one co-owner, the survivor would receive the property. It is extremely essential that the precise language be used in the deed. In a joint tenancy ownership, a co-owner's interest is subjected to actions by his creditors.

Tenancy by the entirety ownership occurs when husband and wife buy property together. In essence, this is a form of ownership that also has the element of right of survivorship. One party acting alone cannot destroy a tenancy by the entirety. The property cannot be sold to satisfy a judgment against the husband or wife acting individually. The property can be sold to satisfy a judgement against both husband and wife for joint obligations. Neither the husband nor wife can dispose of the property by will. Both must agree to convey the property by deed, and signatures of the husband and wife are required on the deed. Homebuyers should be aware of the fact that tenancy by the entirety is not recognized in all states. This form of ownership, however, is recognized in community property states.

Homebuyers must give great consideration to the type of ownership they chose. They should understand the effects of the selected ownership and certainly be in agreement as to how title to property will be received. If they are uncertain about the language used, they should, of course, consult an attorney.

It is of paramount importance that homebuyers be in total agreement on how property is to be distributed. It is best that they consult their attorneys to discuss their plans. The attorneys could then advise the homebuyers on what form of ownership to use and the language to be used in the deed.

DISPOSITION OF PROPERTY ON DEATH OF ONE SPOUSE

JOINT TENANCY

```
                    ┌─────────────┐
                    │    JOINT    │
                    │   TENANCY   │
                    │  WITH RIGHTS│
                    │     OF      │
                    │SURVIVORSHIP │
                    └─────────────┘
```

MARRIED WITH NO CHILDREN	PROPERTY PASSES TO SURVIVING SPOUSE
MARRIED WITH CHILDREN FROM PRESENT AND FROM PREVIOUS UNIONS	ALL TO SURVIVING SPOUSE
	EQUALLY TO SURVIVING CHILDREN IF BOTH PARENTS ARE DECEASED
MARRIED WITH CHILDREN FROM PRESENT UNION	ALL PROPERTY PASSES TO SURVIVING SPOUSE
UNMARRIED WITHOUT CHILDREN	SURVIVING PARENTS EQUALLY DIVIDED
	OR BROTHERS & SISTERS EQUALLY DIVIDED
UNMARRIED WITH CHILDREN FROM PREVIOUS UNIONS	SURVIVING CHILDREN EQUALLY DIVIDED

The joint tenancy ownership form usually can be destroyed in some states by one owner conveying his share to another person. The ownership consequently is converted to a tenants-in-common ownership.

DISPOSITION OF PROPERTY ON DEATH OF ONE SPOUSE

TENANCY IN COMMON

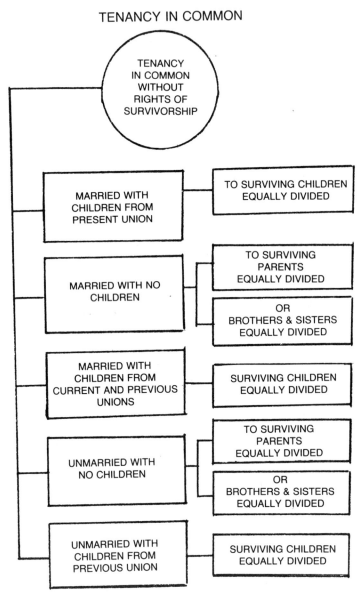

Under a tenancy in common ownership, a co-owner may petition the court to have the property divided and sold. In such a case, the other co-owners would have to sell or be forced to buy the equity of the other co-owners.

7

What to Look for in Conducting Housing Inspections

Many homebuyers, in looking for a home to buy, suffer from the "Home Cosmetics Shock Effect." This is a condition where the homebuyers become overly impressed with fancy wallpaper, mirrored walls, and luxurious chandeliers. These items, although they enhance the appearance of the home, contribute little to the utility or livability of the home. Many sellers are schooled on how to decorate their homes in order to attract buyers. Oftentimes, decoration may have been used to conceal defects that are not readily apparent. Any unusual decorative changes made to the home should command special attention. The more the buyers know about the homes they want to buy, the better their chances will be in getting the sellers to make concessions. It is also imperative for the buyers to make certain that all the defects have been discovered. This information and knowledge will enable the buyers to successfully negotiate the selling price or to include the needed repairs in the sales agreement and escrow instructions. Many buyers have purchased homes after conducting only superficial inspections to find after the close of escrow that the home needs major repairs. It is then too late, in many cases, to have the seller or real estate agency have the repairs made, unless the buyer can prove that a clandestine scheme was used to deliberately conceal the defects. If buyers were convinced through statements made by the seller or real estate agent that certain items were in good operating condition, there may be valid grounds to have the items corrected by the seller or real estate agency.

There are four basis and essential areas that should be covered in conducting home inspections. They are (1) mechanics, (2) structural, (3) electrical system, and (4) plumbing. If these four areas are thoroughly inspected, the homebuyers can avoid problems that might have turned out to be very costly to correct. The average homebuyer can conduct a home inspection so that he will be assured that the home has no major defects that may result in expensive repairs. He should become acquainted with some of the defects that may occur in the four major areas. If the homebuyer is apprehensive about the condition of a home, he may contract with a professional house inspector to ascertain and certify the operating condition of all mechanical devices, the plumbing, electricity, and structural.

Plumbing is one of the most important systems in the home. Repairing or replacing defective parts can be very expensive. The homebuyers should check for leaks in the system. There are several ways of confirming leaks. In multilevel homes, the homebuyers should check the ceilings on the first level for water stains and water damage to ceiling coverings. Very low water pressure could indicate a leak someplace in the plumbing system. All of the devices that use water to operate should be checked to see if they are properly operating and free from water leakages. The plumbing system should have proper drainage. The water should flow freely from all sinks and bathtubs. Slow drainage indicates that impediments may be partially clogging the lines, perhaps roots from plants and other obstacles that have entered the plumbing pipes and sewer lines. The buyers should also check to see if the house is connected to the city sewer line. If the house has a seepage system, it should be checked for proper drainage. The seepage pit or leaching bed should be inspected to see if the sewage is backing up and ponding on the ground. This could indicate that another sewage seepage system needs to be installed.

All equipment that is mechanically operated should be inspected. The refrigeration or evaporative cooling system should be inspected for defects. An abnormally loud noise may indicate compressor problems or a defect in the cooler motor. The homebuyers should request any warranties that the sellers may have on the water heater, heating and cooling equipment, and all kitchen appliances. The water heater should be inspected to determine if it has the proper capacity and is in good operating condition. The hot water heater should require a water heater with a recovery rate of forty or more gallons. The hot water heater should be inspected for leakage and rusting of coils. If the area around the drainage pipe has excessive residual rust or the water is discolored, this may be strong evidence that the water heater has to be repaired or replaced.

The electrical system is another important area that requires complete evaluation. One of the first things to inspect is the service panel. Does it need upgrading? Are there enough circuits for the appliances and equipment? The wiring should be inspected for exposed wires. This could be a serious fire hazard that could be prevented by uncovering electrical defects during the inspection. The service panel should be large enough to accommodate additional circuits in the event other major equipment, such as a swimming pool, or appliances are added

28

to the electrical system. The extra circuits could also be used to prevent overloading of the electrical system.

The structural condition of the house is perhaps the most over-looked area. This is probably due to all the decorative things that can be done to cover obvious housing defects. For example, paneling or luxurious wallpaper could be used to cover cracks, which could indicate defects in the foundation. Expensive and colorful carpet could be used on floors to cover cracks that would otherwise reveal that the house has a settling problem. The condition of the roof should be inspected for deterioration. Things to look for include weather-eroded roofing covering, where asphalt shingles are peeling and damaged, wood shakes missing, and built-up gravel washed away by rainwater, ex-posing the roofing sheathing. The structural strength of the roof should be checked for warping of roofing sheathing. The warping may require a complete new roof. If the home has a fireplace, the metal flashing should be checked for waterproofing around the chimney.

The lack of the proper amount of insulation is responsible for energy waste. A homeowner can decrease the cost of energy by at least 20 percent by increasing the amount of insulation in the attic and weather stripping all openings. The homebuyers should check the depth of the insulation in the attic. This can be done easily by observing the thickness of the insulation located near the attic opening. (See chapter 24 for a typical inspection form that could be used.)

8

Contractual Obligations and the Effects of Contingency Clauses

The ambiguity of the language contained in real estate contracts and agreements has been the source of innumerable disputes that have ended up in litigation. All real estate sales contracts and agreements should be written in descriptive and concise terms to avoid misinterpretation. The buyers should be cautious of real estate contracts that are written by owners who sell their own homes without the assistance of a competent real estate or attorney. Some of the best contracts may have been written by owners; however, the chance of costly mistakes would of course be substantially reduced by having a professional write the contract. If both buyer and seller do not fully understand their contractual obligations, there is a possibility that a major disagreement will evolve that may cause the transaction to be canceled. The language of the contract should explain clearly what events or performances are to be completed. One of the most important aspects of the specific performances is the element of time.

Time and duration in completing a specific obligated performance are of paramount inportance. References should be made to the specific time an event or condition should be completed. This is an area that has been very costly to both buyers and sellers. Emphasis should be placed upon the satisfactory completion of certain performances. Also, penalties should be written into the contract to encourage parties to the contract to perform their contractual obligations in accordance with terms of the contract. If there are no penalties to compel or motivate the parties to perform, they may become indifferent and procrastinate in completing their contractual obligations. To illustrate, Thomas purchased a home, paying a down payment of $6,400. The contract terms stated that 50 percent of the down payment was due upon completion of negotiations and signing of the contract. The balance of the down payment was due at the close of escrow. Thomas and his wife went on vacation, and they spent $2,000. They could not come up with all of the remaining amount of the down payment before the closing date. A penalty provision was written into the contract that allowed the seller to claim the money that was deposited should Thomas fail to complete the down payment contractual obligation. In the above case, the language concerning contractual obligations was clearly depicted. Both Thomas and the seller were aware of the terms of the contract. In this case, Thomas has no valid grounds for litigation. He had an option of going on a vacation or completing his contractual obligations.

Contract disputes also may occur over who pays certain closing costs. Closing costs are paid by both the buyer and the seller. However, through the negotiation process, closing costs normally paid by the seller or buyer may be paid by either party. If this type of agreement develops, those closing costs negotiated should be clearly described in language that prevents ambiguity.

The use of contingency clauses in agreements give flexibility to both the buyer and seller. It must be remembered that unwritten intentions cannot be construed as contractual obligations. All negotiated concessions must be translated into specific and concise language in order to be enforceable. Exceptions would be where concessions and compromises are obtained through coercion or one of the parties to the contract is incompetent to negotiate due to mental impairment, perhaps including addiction to drugs, including alcohol. A contingency clause is used to allow a party to a contract to terminate contractual obligations upon the occurence of events or conditions that are beyond the party's control. Using the previous illustration, assume that Thomas was rejected by the lender because the mortgage payments on the new home caused his housing expense ratio to exceed the lender's required standard. A contingency clause could have been written into the contract that stated the sale would be contingent upon Thomas obtaining financing from Supreme Mortgage Company and the down payment would be returned should Thomas's application for home financing from Supreme Mortgage Company be rejected.

The absence of contingency clauses in contracts could impose serious financial burdens on buyers and sellers. This is one of the most important reasons to have an attorney or real estate agent review or develop the language to cover situations that may occur and prevent either the buyer or seller from fulfilling their contractual obligations. For example, assume that Taylor signed an agreement to purchase a home. Terms of the agreement required Taylor to pay one-half of the down payment upon signing the agreement and the balance at close of escrow. A contingency clause was written to the agreement that stated the sale would be contingent upon the sale of Taylor's present home, which had been sold to Jackson. The sale transaction could not be completed by Jackson because of his serious credit deficiencies. The contingency clause written into the agreement allowed Taylor to cancel the purchase agreement without paying a penalty. The contingency clause in this case averted possible litigation between Taylor and the seller, which could have been very costly. Many contract disputes could be prevented by the buyers and sellers' being aware of conditions that could prevent the sale from closing. Contingency provisions could be written to cover these conditions should they occur. Both buyers and sellers should negotiate for contract concessions concerning contingencies. The intent of a contingency clause may not be specific, which could result in the cancellation of an agreement. To illustrate how the ambiguity of a contingency clause could cause contract disputes, assume that the following contingency clause was written into a purchase **agreement: "The seller agrees to the cancellation of this purchase agreement** should the buyer fail to complete the sale of his present property." Suppose the buyer had two houses on the market for sale. How much time is specified for the buyer to close his sale? Although the contingency clause spells out the event that must occur before the sale can be closed, it does not specify a date when the sale should be completed, nor does it identify the property that is to be sold. Because of the ambiguity of the language and contingency clause, contract disputes may surface. It is therefore extremely important that conditions associated with the sale of the property be thoroughly analyzed. Only then can the proper language be developed to prevent misinterpretation of the buyer's or seller's intentions.

9

Understanding the Closing Process

The closing process is perhaps one of the most misunderstood parts of a real estate sales transactions. It, however, is one of the most important aspects of completing a transaction. The closing process concerns a set of conditions that are imposed on both the buyer and seller. The purpose of the closing is to assure that all conditions set forth by the seller and buyer in the sales agreement have been completed within a specified time frame. A title company or escrow company generally conducts the closing proceedings for a fee. The closing process is an essential part of the sales transaction. It is that segment in which both buyer and seller have complied with conditions and title to the property is conveyed by the seller to the buyer.

The closing agent will carry out all the required functions necessary to close the sale. Both the buyer and seller will be contacted by the closing agent to complete specific performances. The seller may be required to install a new roof or upgrade the plumbing and electrical systems. The buyer may be required to submit the down payment and his share of the closing costs. After these conditions are met, the closing agent will disperse the funds to the seller in exchange for passing title to the buyer. The closing agent will also have the necessary documents recorded as required by law. Federal law requires that the lender provide a good faith estimate of the closing costs. Under this law, the Real Estate Settlement Procedures Act (RESPA), the lender must give the borrower an estimate of the closing costs within three business days. In addition, the law limits the amount that a lender can hold in escrow account for real estate taxes and insurance. The lender must inform both buyer and seller the amount of the closing costs twenty-four hours before closing. This gives the parties time to have their attorneys or other representatives examine the various fees charged for special services. Each service fee can be examined for authenticity and for accuracy.

Following is an itemized list of expenses that are incurred in a real estate transaction. There are certain costs that are traditionally paid by the seller, and buyer. There are no regulations that would prohibit the seller and buyer from paying certain closing costs in order to complete a real estate sales transaction.

Closing Costs

Seller's Expense	Buyer's Expense
Broker Commission	Appraisal
Attorney's Fees	Attorney's Fees
Property Taxes and Assessments	Property Taxes and Assessments
Recording Fees	Recording Fees
Hazard Insurance	Title Insurance
	Hazard Insurance
	Credit Report
	Loan Application Fees
	Survey Fees
	Adjust Interest

THE REAL ESTATE SETTLEMENT PROCEDURES ACT (RESPA)

RESPA is a federal law designed to control the costs incurred in real estate transactions. Lenders are required by this law to supply the buyer and seller an itemized list of the expenses resulting from the fees charged by the closing agent. The law also requires the lender to give the buyer a "good faith estimate" of the closing costs within three days after the homebuyer submits a loan application. The law requires that the lender concurrently give the buyer a copy of the Housing and Urban Development (HUD) publication that interprets and explain the various types of expenses usually incurred in most real estate transactions.

RESPA also provides the homebuyer with the right of examining the final closing cost document within twenty-four hours before the closing date. If there are any discrepancies, the buyer may request that adjustments be made. The buyer is also entitled to a copy of the closing cost document after closing. The RESPA act is very important. It provides protection for the buyer and seller against exorbitant and fraudulent closing fees.

If the buyer intends to use funds provided by a lender to finance the purchase of the home, a provision should be included in the closing documents to allow for the return of the earnest money and down payment in the event the buyer fails to qualify for the loan. This section in the closing documents should be worded carefully. Failure to develop language that clearly depicts how the down payment is to be apportioned should the buyer voluntarily elect to withdraw from the real estate transaction could result in costly litigation. To illustrate how some problems may occur due to the lack of or the ambiguity of the language used for closing the transaction, assume that Franklin purchased a home, paying $8,500 as a down payment. The real estate agent used the following language in the sales agreement: "The buyer understands that should the sales agreement not be completed by a specified date, the down payment shall be retained." This statement is ambiguous and inconclusive. First, the statement does not list conditions under which the down payment will be retained. Second, it does not clearly delineate the seller's responsibilities. What happens should the seller delay in meeting his specific performances? Language must be developed to clearly delineate the outcomes should specific conditions not be complied with by both parties. Poor writing procedures could be avoided by both the buyer and seller holding a conference with their attorneys or real estate brokers to agree on terms and develop the proper language that effectively describes the effects of conditions that prevent the sales from being consummated.

The closing costs are normally paid by the buyer and seller on a proportionate basis. However, either may agree to pay certain expenses. If the closing costs are negotiated by a buyer and seller, those costs that the seller agrees to pay should be clearly identified and described. Many real estate transactions have been canceled because, during the negotiation, concessions were made, but not adequately explained in the closing documents.

10

An Overview of Fair Housing Laws

The Housing Acts of 1954 and 1968 are two of the most important housing acts ever passed. However, in actuality, fair housing laws date back to the 1866 federal statute that prohibited racial discrimination in renting, leasing, buying, or converting any kind of housing. Although some kind of fair housing laws existed over 100 years ago, very few members of minorities benefited from fair housing legislation. Had these laws been enforced effectively, the incidence of black ghettos and Hispanic barrios would be significantly reduced or virtually non-existent. The fact that that they do exist and in large numbers indicates that the previous fair housing laws were ineffective and easily circumvented.

TITLE VII OF THE 1968 FAIR HOUSING LAW

Title VII of the 1968 Fair Housing Law was of paramount importance in removing racial barriers that had prevented members of minorities from moving into predominantly all-white neighborhoods. Section 804 of Title VIII incorporates features that for the first time give fair housing laws the power necessary to correct and remove clandestine schemes designed to circumvent fair housing laws. The following illustrations will delineate how fair housing laws prevent discriminatory schemes from depriving minorities of housing opportunities.

It is illegal to refuse to sell or rent after making a bona fide offer or to refuse to negotiate for the sale or rental of or otherwise make unavailable or deny a dwelling to any person because of race, color, religion, or national origin. If Adams, a black homebuyer, makes a bona fide offer to Smith, a white seller, to purchase his home for the asking sales price, discriminatory charges may be filed if Smith refuses to sell the home and later sells it to Anderson, a white homebuyer, for the same price offered by Adams.

Section 804 also prohibits discrimination against any person in the terms, conditions, or privileges of sale or rental of a dwelling or in the provision of services or facilities in connection with the property because of race, color, religion, or national origin. For example, a land developer or corporation could not sell a condominium to a black home-buyer that impose financial terms, conditions, or privileges that are different from those applied to white homebuyers. If the use of special facilities is contingent upon fees that are not incorporated in the agreements with white homebuyers, there may be valid grounds for discriminatory charges against the seller.

Racial steering is a subtle form of discrimination that is used to prevent members of minorities from buying homes in specific neighborhoods. Under Section 804E, a real estate agent is prohibited from steering minority homebuyers to predominately minority neighborhoods with the intention of reserving homes in white neighborhoods for white homebuyers. Racial steering is very difficult to detect, due to the subtle way it is perpetrated. Statements by a real estate agent that direct minorities to specific neighborhoods may be construed as racial steering. An example is: "Homes in the Moon Shadow Subdivision are financed by lenders who call the loans due when they are sold; they then substantially increase the interest rate on new loans." When the agent subsequently informs the minority homebuyer that special concessions are made on homes located in a predominately minority neighborhood and does not make these same statements to white homebuyers, racial steering may be the underlying motive for such remarks. Racial steering can be confirmed by using testers. This method includes using a white homebuyer to approach the same real estate agent with the intention of buying a home in Moon Shadow Subdivision. If the agent offers to sell a home in Moon Shadow Subdivision to the white homebuyer, the court may construe that the sales agent's actions constitute racial steering, which is a violation of the fair housing law.

The key to detecting racial steering is being able to produce documentation and/or testimonies to show that a minority homebuyer was encouraged and induced to buy in a designated area while the agent denied or used statements to dissuade the purchaser from buying a home that was subsequently offered to white homebuyers. Racial steering decreases the housing opportunities for minorities and causes them to buy homes in predominately minority-occupied neighborhoods.

BLOCKBUSTING AFFECTS NEIGHBORHOOD STABLIZATION AND RESULTS IN PREDOMINATELY IMPACTED MINORITY NEIGHBORHOODS

Section 804E of the 1963 Fair Housing Act makes it illegal for a real estate agent, for profit, to induce or attempt to induce any person to sell or rent an dwelling that will cause the entry or prospective entry into the neighborhood of a person of a particular race or religion. Block-busting means motivating or inducing white homeowners to sell their property before minority homebuyers move into the neighborhood and cause property values to decrease. It may be started by a real estate agent's buying property that is up for sale and renting it or even taking a loss to sell it to a minority homebuyer. When the first member of a minority moves into the neighborhood, white homeowners may begin to panic and list their homes for sale, quite often for less than the market value, which, in effect, causes the property values to decrease. With more and more white homeowners selling their homes at reduced prices, the neighborhood eventually becomes primarily occupied by minority homeowners. Blockbusting can be easily contrived by real estate agents using clandestine schemes. Blockbusting is perpetrated in such a sophisticated way that it is not readily apparent. Even the victims of blockbusting do not realize that they are being manipulated. Once the forces of blockbusting are in operation, a chain reaction occurs to augment the process. There are cases where subdivisions have been virtually transformed from white ownership to predominately minority ownership. This perpetual clandestine racial transformation of neigh-borhoods has caused white homeowners to sell their homes below the fair market values and move farther out to surburban neighborhoods. Many of these homeowners took substantial losses. In some cases, real estate agents purchased the homes at a low price and sold them at the market price, reaping huge profits. Blockbusting can be controlled by white homeowners' recognizing the hidden motives of sales agents making remarks that imply that property values will decrease when members of a minority move into the neighborhood.

11

The Effects of Lenders' Substituting Trust Deeds for Mortgages as Security Instruments

A few years ago, lenders were using mortgages on a wide-scale basis as security for home mortgage loans. They, however, found that it became very costly to foreclose on the homeowners. The trust deed serves the same purpose as the mortgage. It is a security instrument that holds the homebuyers responsible for repayment of the home loan. Since the introduction of the trust deed, lenders have substantially reduced the legal and administrative costs incurred in initiating foreclosure proceedings. They have also reduced the time it takes to dispossess the homebuyers' homes. Under the mortgage, it normally took between six months and eighteen months to foreclose on the delinquent homebuyers and repossess the property. This time has been reduced from 50 to 80 percent. Under the mortgage instrument, the lender was required to obtain a judiciary foreclosure. This normally took a considerable amount of time and involved exorbitant legal, administrative, and court expenses. The trust deed enabled the lender to obtain a nonjudiciary foreclosure, requiring minimal legal costs and no court fees. Under the mortgage, the homebuyers had a redemption period of six months in which they were allowed to redeem the property by paying the entire outstanding mortgage plus costs incurred in obtaining the judiciary foreclosure. There is no redemption period under the trust deed. The homeowner loses his equity in the property if he does not pay all costs incurred by the lender in a nonjudiciary foreclosure prior to the sale of the property as a trustee sale. The trust deed involves three parties: the trustor (borrower), the trustee (the party to whom the property is conveyed as security for the note), and the beneficiary (lender). In case of a default by the trustor, the trustee initiates foreclosure action upon request from the beneficiary under the trustee deed.

FORECLOSURE ACTIONS BY THE TRUSTEE

If the borrower defaults on the trust note, the beneficiary may direct the trustee to commence foreclosure actions. The trustee is required to mail a notice of sale to the borrower within ninety days before the sale. The trustee must also publish the notice of sale for thirty days. The notice must also be served personally on the occupants or posted on the property if it is vacant. After ninety days, the trustee may sell the property at a trustee sale to the highest bidder. The successful bidder gets a trustee deed. The lender saves court expenses and minimizes legal costs. Once the sale is consummated, the homebuyers lose all of his equity and interest in the home. The homeowner does not have the right of redemption. Generally, there is no deficiency judgement, providing the property is a one- or two-family dwelling and on less than two and one-half acres of land. The deficiency judgment is the difference between what the property sold for at the trustee sale and the amount owed on the property at time of the sale. Many homebuyers are under the impression that if the market value of the property exceeds what is actually owed on the home, the lender will submit the difference after the home has been sold. The lender is interested in recapturing his investment. If the bid is lower than the amount owed, the lender will make a higher bid in order to protect his investment. The amount of the bid will be no higher than what is owed on the property. This action would wipe out the homeowner's equity. To illustrate how a homeowner could lose substantial equity in a home, assume that Rogers defaulted on his trust note. After the trustee completed the required procedures to obtain a nonjudiciary foreclosure, the home was put up for sale at a trustee sale. The home had a market value of $65,500. The outstanding mortgage balance was $35,500. The mortgage was six months delinquent, with payments of $350 per month. Late charges must also be considered in the total amount of delinquency that is due on the mortgage loan. Late charges were assessed at fifteen dollars per month. Legal and trustee fees totaled $375. The following schedule shows the total amount due on the delinquent loan.

TOTAL AMOUNT DUE ON DELINQUENT MORTGAGE

Amount Owed on Mortgage	$35,500
Six Months' Delinquent Mortgage Payments	2,100
Six Months' Late Charges	90
Legal and Trustee Fees	375
Total Amount Due on Delinquent Mortgage	$38,065

Since the market value of the home is $65,500 and the total amount due, including delinquent mortgage payments and legal and trustee fees, is $38,065, the total amount of the equity that could be lost by the homeowner if he does not reinstate the mortgage is $27,435 (market value of $65,500 less $38,065 total amount due. The amount due includes delinquent mortgage payments, late charges, and trustee fees.). If the highest bid on the home was $25,500, the lender would submit a higher bid and receive title to the property. The lender could then sell the property for the market value. Since there are no redemption rights in a nonjudiciary foreclosure, there would be no opportunity for Rogers to regain his equity.

The foreclosure problem is more complicated if there is a second loan on the home. Suppose that our friend Rogers used a second mortgage to borrow $8,500 from Faith Mortgage Company. If Rogers defaulted on the second mortgage with Faith Mortgage Company while maintaining the first mortgage in a current state, the home could still be foreclosed. Faith Mortgage Company could go through the nonjudiciary foreclosure process and have the property sold at a trustee sale. Assuming that the total amount due on the second loan, including delinquent payments and other fees, is $7,500 and the highest bid is $6,800, Faith Mortgage Company could submit a higher bid and obtain title to the property. In this case, Rogers would lose $22,500 (This $65,500 market value of the home less $43,000, the amount owed on first and second mortgages). This would be the amount of Rogers's equity after deducting the amount owed on the first and second mortgages.

The lender and trustee are required to follow certain procedures before they can sell the home at a trustee sale. If the procedures are not followed in accordance with state regulations concerning trustee sales, the homeowners have a right to contest the discrepancy in the procedures and methods used by the trustee or lender. The homeowners generally have the right to reinstate the delinquent mortgage by paying all of the delinquent payments, including late charges and expenses incurred by the lender or trustee. Because of the exorbitant legal and trustee fees charged the homeowners, most states have enacted regulations to minimize the cost involved in nonjudiciary foreclosures. Lenders are now using nonjudiciary foreclosures to reduce the cost and time required to obtain title to properties. One of the advantages that trust deeds has over mortgages is that the amount of money needed to reinstate the mortgage is not padded with costly legal fees. Normally, the bids on homes that are sold at trustee sales are smaller than the amount left owning on the homes. If, however, the amount of the bid is greater than the amount owing on the home, the net proceeds will be disbursed to cover: (1) the costs and expenses incurred in selling the property, including the trustee's and attorney's fees, (2) the payment of the contract secured by the trust note, (3) the payment to junior lienholders or other encumbrances in order of their priority, and (4) the payment to trustor (homeowner), should any funds remain after paying all encumbrances on the home. The homeowner who stands to lose substantial equity in the home as a result of a foreclosure should not trust the bid process; he should make every effort to reinstate the mortgage prior to the sale of the home at a trustee sale.

NOTICE OF TRUSTEE'S SALE

NOTICE IS HEREBY GIVEN pursuant to A.R.S. 833-808 that the following described real property will be sold, pursuant to the power of sale under that certain deed of trust recorded in docket or book _____ at page _____ records of _____ County, at public auction to the highest bidder on:

DATE: _____ , 19 _____ , TIME _____

ADDRESS: _____ of Maricopa

Legal Description:

_____

Name of Trustor in Said Deed of Trust:

_____

_____

Dated this _____ day of _____ , 19 _____ .

_____
BY Trustee .

STATE OF _____
COUNTY OF _____

This instrument was acknowledged before me this _____ day ____ of _____ , 19 _____

by _____ as an officer of _____

an _____ Corporation, on behalf of the Corporation.

_____
Notary Public
My Commission Expires: _____

42

12

What the Homeowner Should Know about Financial Management and Dept-Income Controls

The success of businesses depends heavily on the effectiveness of established financial management and debt control measures. 'Like a business, a homeowner should have sound fiscal policies under which to manage household expenditures. The lack of financial controls has caused many homeowners to overspend, resulting in the misappropriation of family incomes.

To prevent debts from mounting, homeowners should develop and implement various financial controls. This will allow the homeowners to identify problem areas requiring fiscal adjustments and modifications.

There are numerous financial strategies that can be designed to achieve a high degree of financial stability. Once these strategies have been developed, the homeowners should adhere strongly to the restraints and policies.

One of the most effective management strategies that should be installed as part of the homeowner's overall financial control plans is developing a logical and reasonable forecasting schedule. Business corporations have controlled cash flow problems effectively and improved their debt-income ratios by using financial forecasting. Homeowners can use this same management technique to maintain and enhance fiscal stability. In order to incorporate financial forecasting in his fiscal control plan, the homeowner must have a clear perception of his financial capacity. He must also understand the effect that uncontrolled household variable expenses can have on financial management plans. Financial forecasting means projecting the occurrence of anticipated expenditures and establishing a savings plan to pay them as they come due without incurring additional debts. Some homeowners do not plan for future expenditures, such as vacations, Christmas, auto repairs, and school. They allow these costly events to occur without making appropriate financial preparations. If no provisions are made for paying the costs of these occurrences, the homeowner will be confronted with the financial dilemma of borrowing money or using money that has been set aside for other financial obligations.

The obligation most likely to be selected by the homeowner as a financial tradeoff is the mortgage payment. One of the reasons the mortgage payment is selected is because it is generally the largest monthly cash payment that is made by the homeowner. Substantial money can be accumulated over a short period of time. One homeowner stated that he pays for his family vacation every year with his mortgage payments. A large sum of money can be accumulated by missing three mortgage payments. For example, if a homeowner's monthly mortgage payment is $575, if the homeowner fails to pay three mortgage payments, he could accumulate a debt of $1,725. The amount of money equal to three mortgage payments is normally enough to cover many major household expenses, such as a vacation or major auto repairs. The homeowner should realize this method of paying for a vacation or other household expenses indicates very poor financial management.

Another reason the mortgage payment is used is because the collection methods utilized by mortgage lenders are not as intimidating and aggressive as those used by collection agencies. The homeowner does not have to worry about a collection agent driving his home away, as he could a car, because of delinquent payments. Since neighbors do not know when the homeowner mortgage is delinquent, he will not become embarrassed, as he would be if a collection agent repossessed his car. But the homeowner will have to borrow money to eliminate the mortgage delinquency that was created when the mortgage payments were converted to other uses and purposes.

Debt control requires that the homeowner establish control over household variable expenses. These expenses, if allowed to increase, can reduce the homeowner's disposable income and affect his ability to pay other obligations. Fixed household expenses cannot be controlled by the homeowner; however, variable expense is an area that can be significantly modified to change the debt income structure. Examples of variable expenses are utilities, travel, food, and recreation. Each of the preceding expenses should be scrutinized carefully. The homeowner may be able to reduce the level of spending by controlling household variable expenses.

The homeowner can create substantial savings by reducing the level of energy consumption by requesting an energy audit from the utility company. The homeowner can identify energy saving measures that can be used to reduce utility bills. One homeowner found that weather-stripping and the increase of attic insulation decreased his utility bill by twenty percent. Energy consumption can be an effective financial management tool to increase disposable income.

It is necessary for the homeowner to adhere strongly to financial restraints once the variable expenses have been modified and projected. The controlling of variable expenses should be one of the key financial strategies used by the homeowner to improve financial management plans. They are of paramount importance and must be greatly emphasized as areas requiring the greatest adjustments. Household variable expenses are the easier expenses to control from an accounting perspective but they sometimes become extremely difficult when the homeowner places more value on the social aspect of impressing his neighbors.

The lack of the ability to develop financial management skills and implement a rigid debt control system has caused the breakup of many marriages. The irony of this condition is that these homeowners are generally not aware of the detrimental impact that serious financial problems can have on relationships. The homeowner could also overact by becoming too frugal, using unnecessarily repressive financial restraints that could significantly reduce the family's standard of living.

As mentioned before, debt consolidation is a common practice that homeowners use to control their debts. This method, however, can be used inappropriately. Debt consolidation may work for some, but may not be necessary for others. Before deciding to use debt consolidation as a financial management strategy, the homeowner should determine the projected increase in cash flow and the amount of the balance and the time remaining on the loans. For example, if the homeowner has six different debts with less than twelve months or less remaining on the bills, there will generally be no financial benefits in consolidating the debts.

13

How to Maintain the Proper Debt-Income Ratio

Maintaining the proper debt-income ratio is no easy task for the extravagant homeowner. He generally is not concerned about where his money is being spent. He has extremely poor financial management skills. Improper debt-income ratios have caused many homeowners to lose their homes through foreclosure. It is only when a financial disaster occurs that many homeowners become seriously concerned about debt-income ratios. In many cases, they have gotten so far in debt and the magnitude of the debts gives them very few options to correct their financial problems.

Maintaining a proper debt-income ratio can be achieved by using certain precautious to prevent conditions that lead to high debt-income ratios and by developing an effective financial management plan to control and reduce the debts to an affordable level.

One of the first things the homeowner should do to control his debts is make a realistic evaluation of his spending habits and living style. One or both of these areas may require serious adjustments and modifications.

The second task, and perhaps the most important, is defining or identifying a debt-income ratio that will be commensurate with a modified and adjusted living style. Many mortgage lenders use a debt-income ratio of 36 percent of gross income to qualify homebuyers. Others use a lower or higher percentage, dependent upon individual circumstances. Many economic advisers and credit counselors think that 36 percent of the gross income is too high for some families. Using 36 percent as a debt-income ratio would mean that a family with a combined income of $3,500 per month could not have debts in which the total monthly installments exceeded $1,260. This amount includes the total housing expenses, plus expenses for all charge accounts and auto payments. If the homeowner lacks financial management and budgetary skills, it is recommended that a more safer and conservative debt-income ratio such as 30 percent of gross income be used.

The major problem with high debt-income ratios is that no financial flexibility is available to take care of household emergencies. To show how easy it is to inadvertently create high debt-income ratios, assume that the Logan family has a gross income of $3,200 per month. Expenses and financial obligations include the following; mortgage payment, $675; utilities, $150; property taxes, $40; hazard insurance, $25; mortgage insurance, $20; six charge accounts, $475; two cars with monthly payments of $325 and $250; and a boat that costs $175 per month. In addition, Logan pays $135 per month for insurance on the two cars. The total of the monthly installments is $2,270. This represents 71 percent of his gross income, which is a serious and dangerously high debt-income ratio. A household emergency could cause a financial disaster for the Logan family. He should develop and implement corrective measures to reduce the critically high debt-income ratio immediately.

One way to reduce critical debt-income ratios is increasing the income. This can be done by using various methods. A common method is obtaining temporary or part-time employment. This method is probably the most practical, and it is used widely by homeowners. The one big disadvantage of this method is that oftentimes, the additional income generated from part-time or temporary employment is used to incur additional debts. By using the income only to reduce the current debt level, the homeowner could substantially decrease the debt-income ratio and reach a debt level that would improve his financial structure. This solution will provide only temporary relief to the homeowners if they persist in using the same spending habits that got them in debt and fail to develop an effective financial management plan.

Liquidating assets can also reduce the debt-income ratio. The biggest obstacle to asset liquidation is the homeowner's pride. From his perspective he has failed to achieve an acceptable standard of living. He also becomes aware of his neighbors' impressions and is concerned about what they would think if they saw a "for sale" sign on the boat or second car. Asset liquidation has a dual effect on the homeowner's income structure. It increases the disposable income while reducing the excessive financial obligations. In some cases where large monthly obligations are responsible for the high debt-income ratios, their elimination alone may be sufficient to put the family on sound fiscal grounds. Therefore, it is important to make an accurate financial analysis of the homeowner's debt-income structure.

The best fiscal policy is to use the corrective measures that have the greatest impact on changing the debt-income ratio without drastically affecting the homeowner's welfare. The financial strategies used should result in the greatest debt reduction over the shortest period of time. This may entail employing a combination of methods in order to maximize their impact. The types and combination of financial management techniques used should be incorporated into the plans and determined by size and duration of the financial obligations. Debt consolidation can also be an effective technique that can be used to control and reduce the debt-income ratio. This method, however, has caused many homeowners to aggravate their financial problems instead of eliminating them. There have been cases where homeowners consolidated their debts to reduce their financial obligations, and six months later, these same homeowners found themselves in a more precarious financial situation requiring additional long-term credit counseling. To prevent a financial disaster, the debt-income structure can be changed or modified, but this requires the use of the three Financial Ds of Diligence in adherence to budgets designed to achieve fiscal stability, Discipline in controlling spending habits and modifying lifestyles, and Dedication in developing financial management skills and applying them in a positive manner to achieve financial security and solvency. High debt-income ratios, unless controlled by the homeowners, will cause financial conditions that could force the homeowners into bankruptcy. These conditions should be corrected and a financial management plan designed to prevent their recurrence. Above all, homeowners should take a closer look at their living styles. This is the area that has caused many of their financial problems. It is also the area in which homeowners experience the most difficulties adjusting.

14

How to Improve Your Credit

A person with a very good credit rating can be considered to have a valuable intangible asset. Practically all consumer goods and services are purchased with credit cards and installment accounts. The national debt is a very good example of how important credit is to consumers. Banks, savings and loan associations, and even credit unions spend millions of dollars promoting the use of Master and VISA cards. Some credit unions encourage consumers to expand their financial obligations by conducting contests where sweepstakes tickets are given to consumers in accordance with the amount of money they have borrowed. Monetary prizes as well as television sets and vacations are given as prizes to those who have winning tickets. It is becoming difficult to rent a car or check into a hotel without a major credit card. All of these examples are credit market strategies that are designed to encourage consumers to expand their credit capacities.

Poor credit ratings and credit deficiencies are caused by three essential factors: (1) reduction or loss of income, (2) inadequate financial management skills, or (3) extravagant living styles. Loss of income may be caused by divorce, loss of employment, or death. Loss of income, regardless of the reason, creates the most devastating impact on the financial ability of consumers to maintain their debts in a current state. To protect the credit rating, the consumers must make major changes in their debt-income structure to compensate for the substantial loss in income. Debt consolidation and the liquidation of assets should be considered. These two strategies could reduce or eliminate financial obligations that, if not paid, could cause serious credit problems and deficiencies. The lack of financial management skills is responsible for many derogatory credit reports. This is a problem that can be corrected by using a budget to control variable and fixed expenses. By using the budget, the consumer can eliminate the overspending problem, thereby increasing the cash flow. The budget will assist the consumer in improving financial management skills that can be used to establish financial controls. Extravagent living styles cause the consumers to create excessive financial obligations that result in credit deficiencies. By adjusting the living style, consumers can bring their debt-income ratio into the proper balance. They will increase their disposable incomes, which will allow them to pay monthly debts on time, hence eliminating the slow credit deficiency. Delinquent installment accounts could be brought up to date by using the increase in disposable income to pay delinquent accounts. Extravagant living styles can affect the consumers' credit record in two ways: (1) They cause a disproportionate percentage of the income to be committed to financial obligations, which causes the accounts to become delinquent. (2) Although the consumers may be current with all debts, the debt-income ratio may be excessive. In this case, the consumer is financially overextended. If the consumer wanted to obtain a loan for a car or other household goods, the loan application may be rejected.

Poor credit ratings are caused by the following four major credit actions that are initiated against consumers by creditors: (1) collection accounts, (2) charge-offs, (3) judgments, and (4) slow credit.

Collection accounts are difficult to correct because of the third-party involvement. The creditor will normally assign delinquent accounts that he has been unable to collect to collection agencies. This creates a third-party collection situation where the collection agency's primary objective is getting the consumer to pay off the delinquent account. It receives a percentage of the outstanding delinquent accounts. Therefore, it is difficult to get the collection agency to cooperate in removing the collection account deficiency from the credit reports. It is, therefore, extremely important for consumers to pay the delinquent accounts before they are assigned to collection agencies by creditors. It would be to the advantage of the consumers to pay the creditors off in full and request that the deficiency be removed from their credit report. All communications with the creditors concerning derogatory credit should be with the credit manager. He would probably be the only person with the authority to request the collection agencies and credit reporting agencies to remove the deficiencies from the consumers' credit reports. The consumers should submit documentation depicting the reasons for their credit problems. The most convincing documentation would be correspondence from doctors and employers explaining conditions that resulted in the reduction of the consumers' incomes and were beyond their control. Credit deficiencies will remain on the credit report for five or more years. Therefore, it would be advantageous for the consumers to try to get the derogatory credit items completely removed from their credit reports. It is very important that the consumers communicate only with employees who are in administrative capacities, not account clerks and credit counselors. It is also essential for consumers to submit justification letters to the credit reporting agency explaining the conditions and circumstances that caused the credit deficiencies.

Charge-offs are delinquent accounts that have been reported to a credit reporting agency by the creditor. They are accounts that the creditors have written off as bad debts and uncollectable. Charge-offs are one of the easiest credit deficiencies to correct. The consumer can correct the deficiency by reinstating the account or paying the entire balance. In either case, the credit manager should be requested to have the derogatory account removed from the consumer's credit report. Once the charge-off accounts are reactivated, the consumer should keep them current by paying several months ahead. It is also important for the consumer to pay more than the actual amount due on the debt. This plan will show that the consumer is trying to establish credibility and a pattern of consistent payments.

Correcting judgments is much more involved and requires that the consumer communicate with the creditors' attorneys. It is important that the consumers submit documentation to show that conditions beyond their control created financial problems that made it difficult to pay off the debt. Judgments are obtained through the courts because judgments usually involve larger sums of money. The most effective way of correcting judgments is to pay off the judgment or make arrangements with the creditors to pay the loan by using a formalized repayment plan. The repayment plan should be prepared carefully, with due dates and amounts specified. The plan is more likely to be accepted by the creditors if the language states that all payments will be submitted with certified funds in the form of money orders or cashier's checks. The plan would also create a favorable impact if it was signed and notarized. The judgment may be deleted from the credit report by having the creditor's credit manager or someone in a higher position submit a written request to the credit reporting agency requesting the judgment be deleted.

Slow credit occurs when consumers become overextended with financial obligations or fail to establish financial controls over debts. Like charge-offs, slow credit is easy to correct. The first thing the consumer should do is submit a justification letter to the creditor explaining the reasons for the slow credit. This letter should be supported by documentation of the conditions disclosed in the justification letter. The slow credit could be eliminated by the consumer's developing a consistent pattern of payments, with the installments made before they are due. Slow payment can be prevented by the consumer's initiating actions to reduce the debt-income ratios. They cause the consumer to misappropriate monthly installment funds, which results in a consistent pattern of slow payments. By reducing the debt-income ratio to below 40 percent, the consumer will eliminate the cash flow problem. Additional funds would be available to bring the delinquent accounts current. Establishing fiscal restraints in spending may also create enough disposable income to be used to increase the monthly installments on the delinquent accounts. Cutbacks in spending should be carefully considered as a method to control slow credit. In many cases, extravagent spending and compulsive buying are the primary reasons for slow credit.

HOW TO REESTABLISH DAMAGED CREDIT

Reestablishing credit reliability can be a difficult and arduous task for many consumers. This task, however, is not impossible to accomplish. It does take ingenuity and an effective, well-delineated plan to eliminate credit deficiencies. Some of the deficiencies may be eliminated or deleted from the consumer's credit reports. They can be substantially mitigated by applying certain appropriate actions. Most consumers are under the impression that once credit is damaged, nothing can be done to improve it. This is a false belief. There are numerous methods of improving poor credit ratings or reestablishing damaged credit.

The consumer may be able to reestablish Mastercard and VISA accounts by using the pledge account approach. This method requires the consumer to make an initial deposit to the bank, credit union, or savings and loan association. The amount of money would be dependent upon the agreement between the bank and the consumer. It may be accomplished with $1000 or perhaps a lower amount. The concept of the pledge account approach is based on offsetting funds to compensate for purchase made by the consumers. Each purchase that is made by the consumer is offset by funds in the pledge account. By making purchases and paying on a very consistent basis, the consumer can reestablish credit reliability. To enhance the credit rating further, the consumer should pay installments every two weeks. Following this plan shows that the consumer is paying on a consistent basis. The purpose of this plan is improving or reestablishing the consumer's credit. Therefore, the pledge account should not be used extensively.

Opening mail order accounts is another way of reestablishing damaged credit. The important thing is not to overspend in reestablishing credit. Some consumers use ingenious plans, but find that they have overextended their financial capacity. This will aggravate the credit problem, making it difficult to correct or reestablish one's credit rating.

15

Distressed Equity Acquisition by Liquidation through Buying Distressed Property

Buying homes from distressed property owners can create instant equity for a wise and knowledgeable homebuyer. This is an approach that many of the "Get Rich Quick," seminars are using to induce people to enroll in their seminars. These seminars lead a buyer to believe that it is easy to buy a home with no credit and no money down. It can be done—in fact, it is done quite frequently—however, certain conditions and circumstances have to prevail for the no-money down–and-no-credit concept to work.

Many buyers have the erroneous impression that distressed property is a deteriorated and dilapidated home located in a neighborhood that consists mainly of run-down homes. This is a terribly misconstrued impression. Distressed homes fall into a broad spectrum of values, ranging from deteriorating structures in depressed neighborhoods to palatial homes located in neighborhoods that have homes with market values exceeding $100,000. The location of a home does not cause it to become distressed property. It is the social and financial condition of the homeowner that cause the property to be classified as distressed property. The buyer must also be aware of the fact that just because a distressed property is located in a neighborhood containing homes with high market values, it could be less attrative financially than a home located in a less prestigious neighborhood. The buyer or investor should make a complete assessment of the neighborhood and note if property values are increasing or relatively stable. Distressed property is not a new commodity, as many of the "Get Rich Quick" real estate seminars often suggest. Property owners become distressed sellers because of a multitude of economic and social reasons. Hence there will always be distressed property available to buy. A wise homebuyer or investor in possession of certain kinds of information, such as the trend of market values in a given neighborhood and the motivating factors that are inducing the property owner to sell the property, can capitalize on the unfortunate circumstances that affect the property owners.

Distressed properties may be described as those properties owned by individuals who, because of economic and social circumstances, are forced to sell to prevent further aggravation of their problems.

Economic problems fall into many categories. However, the primary factor is a drastic reduction in income that forces the property owner into a precarious financial situation. Examples of conditions that cause a substantial reduction in income are underemployment or unemployment, death of one of the co-mortgagors, divorce, and financial mismanagement of debts and income. In each of the preceding conditions, a loss or reduction of income will invariably lead to a distressed property sale.

Unemployment is perhaps one of the leading causes of distressed property sales. Once an individual becomes unemployed, the financial capacity to sustain the mortgage in a current state is jeopardized and the owner may be forced to sell the property to preserve some of the equity that has been accumulated. In a divorce, income is generally lost because one of the co-mortgagors vacates the property. The co-mortgagor in possession of the property may not retain the financial capacity to make the monthly mortgage payments. For example, assume that James and Alma purchased a home two years ago with a mortgage payment of $725 per month. James's monthly income was $1,500. Alma earns $1,225 per month. They began to have marital problems and finally went through divorce proceedings. Alma wanted the house and auto and, through court order, was awarded both the home and the car, under the stipulation that she also was to make the $225 monthly payment on the car. James was ordered to pay $200 per month support for their small child. Close scrutiny of Alma's conditions clearly show that she cannot afford the home and will invariably be forced to sell the home at some future date unless her income increases to accommodate the substantial reduction in income due to the divorce, even though Alma has a total monthly income of $1,425, including the $200 per month child support. The mortgage payment alone represents over 50 percent of her income. When the utilities and auto payment are added, the monthly income is reduced to an unmanageable level. This illustration depicts a distressed situation that could be compounded and aggravated should other financial problems arise to increase the magnitude of the financial problems.

The extent of investment that is made in buying property is contingent upon the types and number of concessions that the buyer successfully negotiates with the distressed seller. These concessions are dependent on who the sellers are and how they are classified. Concessions range from the compromised, to the propitious, to utopian, each of which is made by specific distressed sellers.

54

Utopian concessions are those that are extremely advantageous to the buyer such as a willingness on part of the seller to make special financial arranagements that require the buyer to put virtually little or no money down to complete the sales transaction. Propitious concessions are those that the distressed seller is willing to make that require the buyer to make some minor compromises. An example would be where the buyer agrees to pay a small down payment and agrees to assume a first and second mortgage.

Compromise concessions generally are more difficult to negotiate and require a skillful buyer or real estate agent to obtain. These distressed sellers are reluctant to change the terms of their sales offer. However, many of them are operating under a time constraint and may be willing to make certain concessions if the buyer is deliberate, disciplined, and patient.

Distressed property owners can be divided into three basis types: (1) mildly distressed, (2) moderately distressed, and (3) severely distressed. Knowing what type of seller the distressed property owner is will put the buyer in an advantageous negotiating position.

The mildly distressed seller may have to sell. However, money may not be the motivating factor. The seller may have to sell because his place of employment is being changed to another city. Inconvenience more than money may be of paramount importance to the seller. However, because of this inconvenience, the distressed seller may be willing to make utopian and propitious concessions. The buyer, in this case, should be diplomatically assertive in requesting certain concessions, including financial arrangements. Mildly distressed sellers normally are more patience and are not in a financial dilemma where they must sell to avoid an inminent financial catastrophe. Hence the buyer must approach the seller from the time and inconvenience perspective. The mildly distressed seller is usually cognizant of his condition and has considered the ramifications. He can be convinced to make some generous concessions as long as they are not overexaggerated.

The moderately distressed seller is one who is affected by one or more social and/or economic factors. These factors may emerge collectively and intensify the seller's problems, which could cause him to make utopian concessions in order to complete the sale. The moderately distressed seller generally is operating within a tight time frame. The longer it takes to negotiate a sale, the more aggravating the problems and conditions become. If the seller continue to reject sales offers, he risks losing all of the equity that has been accumulated in the property through foreclosure.

Moderately distressed sellers can be identified through their eagerness and willingness to make concessions. Although their behavior is deceptive and they may display an indifferent attitude, time is a factor that will eventually force them to make many concessions. An example of the moderately distressed seller is one who has experienced a drastic reduction in income because of a divorce, loss or reduction of employment, death of one income-producing co-mortgagors, or the incurring of extensive financial obligations that have substantially reduced the seller's cash flow. All of these conditions are generally beyond the seller's control and cause him to make many favorable concessions to the buyer.

The severely distressed seller is one who is ruled by emotions and can easily be talked into making many concessions. These are sellers who, because of conditions that are beyond their control, must immediately sell their property to avoid financial collapse. There has been a substantial reduction in income, with no immediate possibility of restoring it to a level that would enable them to continue making mortgage payments. The severly distressed seller is caught in a situation where he may be forced to share a substantial part of his equity to avoid a total loss of accumulated equity and serious damage to his credit. The buyer is in an advantageous position from which he can get the seller to make many favorable financial arrangements. The "no money down" approach can be effectively utilized, providing either the buyer or seller has the credit and financial capacity to obtain a second mortgage on the property. Many of the "Get Rich Quick" real estate seminars lead the buyer or investor to believe that it is easy to purchase a home even if you have poor, perhaps including a bankruptcy, or no credit rating, and with no money down. This scenario is an exception rather than a rule. It can be accomplished, but not as readily and easily as depicted by the "Get Rich Quick" seminars. One common method or strategy that is often used to purchase a home with no money down and no credit is finding a severely distressed seller who is entering into or has completed divorce proceedings where the court has ordered the property to be sold as part of the divorce dissolution and settlement. These types of distressed sellers often care very little about the equity in the property as long as the other hostile spouse doesn't get it. He or she can be convinced to take out a second loan on the home in order to expedite the sale and get some of the equity out of the home rather than lose it as a result of foreclosure. The severely distressed seller often leaves 10 to 20 percent equity in the home for the buyer, who would then assume the first and second mortgage without paying any money down or needing good credit to qualify. In essence, the buyer has obtained a 100 percent loan with no money down and no credit. In addition, the buyer has obtained instant equity in the property.

Where are these distressed sellers? Locating them is the key factor that makes the no-credit–and–no-money-down concept work. There are numerous places where the distressed sellers can be found. A disciplined buyer who is willing to look for and follow up on leads can generally find many in the divorce notices that are published in the newspapers. The real estate section of the newspaper also has leads that can be followed. Leads, however, must be carefully evaluated. Otherwise, the buyer could spend countless hours chasing blind leads. The following advertisement was taken from a daily newspaper: "DESPERATE OWNER: Has $35K Equity in 4BR, 2½ Ba Home. Assume loan at 11%, Will trade." The preceding ad may or may not lead to a no-money down transaction. Two things are obvious. There are two possible factors that may induce the seller to make utopian or propitious concessions. There is an inconvenience factor of trying to take care of the property. There is also a potential financial factor. The property may remain vacant for several months, causing the seller to simultaneously pay two mortgage payments. It could also be vandalized, which could be costly to the seller.

Banks, mortgage companies, and savings and loan associations are also sources that can be checked for distressed sellers. However, because of the confidentiality factor about disclosing pertinent information about their delinquent mortgagors, the buyer may find few leads. The county tax assessor in each state often posts the names of homeowners whose property is in danger of being sold to satisfy unpaid taxes. By following up on these leads, the buyer may find that these property owners may be experiencing financial problems and are willing to make concessions in the form of generous financial sales arrangements. The buyer or investor can also locate leads on distressed sellers by conducting a survey of the neighborhoods in which they want to buy. By driving through the neighborhoods, the buyer will find many "For Sale by Owner" signs. Some of these property owners may not be knowledgeable about the various financing methods, hence it is essential that the buyer or investor make a realistic assessment of why the owner want to sell. The buyer's approach and the concessions negotiated will be contingent upon the seller's financial and social conditions.

The preceding strategies will not work if the lender has a Due-on-Sale clause in the mortgage note that forces the buyer to obtain new financing with a higher rate of interest. If the buyer is not credit-worthy, he has to rely upon the seller's credit and financial capacity to make the financial arrangements to close the transaction.

16

Condominiums as Alternatives to Single-Family Homes

The high cost of housing and interest rates have eliminated many prospective homebuyers from the housing market. The average cost of a home exceeds $85,000. Hence the American dream of owning a home is an impossibility for thousands of families. The condominium is one of many attempts by the housing industry to make home ownership affordable and a reality for homebuyers falling within certain income brackets. Many apartments are currently being converted to condominiums to attract the homebuyers that find the multifamily housing concept attractive. A condominium is a group of housing units that have common walls and roofs. Each unit is owned individually. Each owner also owns a proportionate share of the common areas. Condominiums are operated by a board consisted of condominium owners. Each condominium owner automatically becomes a member of the condominium owners association and can vote on how the condominium is managed and operated. Condominiums have both disadvantages and advantages. The homebuyer should make a complete assessment of his housing needs before buying a condominium. He should consult with a condominium owner to get an understanding of some problems that are common to condominium owners. The homebuyer will enjoy many benefits that are not available to buyers of single-family homes. The price of a condominium generally is lower than that of a similar single-family home. In addition, condominium owners have access to other amenities, such as tennis courts, saunas, clubhouses, and swimming pools, which provide condominium residents with recreation facilities that would generally be at additional cost to the owner of a single-family home. Perhaps the most important convenience to condominium owners is freedom from outside maintenance and yard work. In fact, this is one of the most important marketing features used by developers to promote the sales of condominiums. The owners can spend the time normally spent maintaining yards for other vocational interests. The disadvantage of this, however, is that owners have no control over the cost of maintenance and have to pay a proportionate share of the increase in the cost of maintenance.

CONDOMINUMS OFFER HOMEBUYERS
A CAREFREE LIVING STYLE

Condominiums are becoming extremely popular and attract first-time homebuyers and those who dislike doing yard work. Other advantages include lower purchase price and amenities such as recreational rooms, saunas, and pools. These amenities would cost individual homeowners thousands of dollars for installation.

All condominums have a paid staff who maintain the common areas. The condo owner has to maintain his own assigned space.

Condominum owners sometimes have access to swimming pools and saunas. These are two major amenities that are found in many condominum complexes. Condominiums provide excellent recreational facilities to owners and their guests.

CONDOMINIUMS OPERATE UNDER
A DECLARATION AND BYLAWS

The operations of condominiums are carried out by the bylaws of the association that have been created by the declaration. The declaration is the most important document that control condominium operations. It is often called the master deed, and covenants and restrictions, or the declaration of conditions. The declaration must be recorded to create single-deed condominium estates. The declaration is the document that creates authority and power through bylaws to allow the board of directors of the association to operate the condominiums. The bylaws created by the declaration allows the board of directors of the association to assess and collect sufficient funds to maintain the common areas. It also provides for legal enforcement of unpaid monthly association fees and special assessments. The enforcement against individual condominium owners is carried out by the association's obtaining liens against individual estates.

The declaration will also delineate the formula used in determining the undivided interest percentage. This is a ratio of a unit to the total of all units. The formula used to determine the undivided interest in common estates of the complex will also affect the following: (1) the amount assessed owners for maintenance and operation of all common areas, (2) the amount of the real estate tax, and (3) the number of votes or voting strength that owners have.

Homebuyers should have a good understanding of the bylaws and how they are affected by the rules and bylaws covenants. Following is a list of some bylaws that affect the rights and responsibilities of condominium owners and tenants: (1) rules for using recreation facilities, (2) for collection of monthly fees and special assessments, (3) for enforcement of liens for unpaid fees and assessments, (4) for use of dwelling units for residential purposes, (5) controlling conditions and conduct that protect and preserve the aesthetic appearance of the development, and (6) concerning the creation of an operating budget to effectively manage the operations of the condominiums. These are only a few examples of basic rules that are contained in condominium bylaws.

COMMON REPAIRS CAN BE COSTLY
FOR CONDOMINUM OWNERS

One of the most costly expenses to affect condominium owners is major structural repairs. Because condominiums are built together, sharing load-bearing walls and plumbing systems, repairs cannot be made on one without affecting others, except for internal repairs to devices not depending on the condominium common systems. If, for example, one owner in a fourplex condominium has a leaking roof, the entire roof, including the portion of three abutting units, may have to be replaced, even though the other dwellings have no leaks. Condominium owners, thereby, have no choice in postponing needed repairs once the governing body decides that repairs are needed. Nor do the owners have a choice in selecting the company that is contracted to perform the rehabilitation work. Condominium owners may also be faced with plumbing problems due to defective plumbing in an abutting unit. Although condominiums have their own individual interior plumbing systems, these systems often are connected to one main drainage line. Therefore if one condominium owner becomes careless and cause the main drain line to clog, eventually all units connected to the main drain will be affected. The plumbing problem could be compounded because of the sewage load imposed on the clogged sewage line from all units in the complex. If someone uses the shower or washer in an abutting condominium, the waste water could back up into other condominiums. Since the problem is common to all the units in the complex, there may be bylaws that require all owners to share in the expense of making the repairs. Normally, condominium owners are responsible for all internal repairs to their units. They would then have the right to select the licensed repairman of their choice.

Prospective condominium buyers should understand what improvements can be made to the unit. Most associations have provisions that place restrictions on the types of improvements that can be made. The owners must get permission before any changes to the outside of the condominium are made.

17

What the Homebuyer Should Know about Mortgage Delinquency and Default

Homebuyers must be aware of financial conditions that affect their ability to maintain the mortgage in a current state. This section will focus upon those areas in which the homeowner can control to miminize and or eliminate to prevent chronic mortgage delinquency.

One of the major causes of mortgage delinquency and default is a reduction in or loss of income. This usually is the result of several events. Unemployment is perhaps one of the most common reasons for mortgage delinquency. If the homeowner has not made provisions for saving on a regular basis, the delinquency may be more difficult to resolve.

A divorce will also affect the ability of a homeowner to maintain the mortgage. Oftentimes, the spouse in possession of the home is under the impression that he or she can maintain the mortgage. However, the loss of one income frequently imposes a financial burden on the spouse in possession of the home. Unless the income is increased, the spouse could become delinquent with the mortgage and eventually lose it through foreclosure.

Co-mortgagors who quit claims the home to the ex-spouse are under the impression that they no longer have any responsibility for the mortgage note. This is an erroneous impression. The co-mortgagor must get a novation from the lender to be released from liability. This document contains a release clause and is used to substitute a new mortgage obligation for a prior mortgage obligation. Generally, both co-mortgagors, the husband and wife, qualified for the house by using joint income. The divorce splits this income. The custodial co-mortgagor, the spouse in possession of the home, may replace the lost income by obtaining part-time employment or by sharing the home with a tenant. Refinancing the home to buy out the ex-spouse's equity could aggravate an existing financial problem. To compensate for the reduction in income, the co-mortgagor in possession should significantly modify his or her living style.

THE EFFECTS OF EXTENSIVE FINANCIAL OBLIGATIONS
ON A HOMEOWNER'S ABILITY TO SUSTAIN A MORTGAGE

Many homeowners automatically program themselves for mortgage delinquency. This occurs when the homebuyer fails to exercise good financial controls over his debts and income. Factors contributing to excessive financial obligations develop quickly. These factors include abusing credit by obtaining too many credit cards. Overextending causes the cash flow to diminish. This loss in income because of excessive financial obligations results in mortgage delinquency and, eventually, foreclosure.

Homeowners must establish spending habits that do not contribute to waste of financial resources. Spending must be controlled so that homeowners can avoid creating extensive financial obligations that will jeopardize their ability to maintain the mortgage. First-time homebuyers and extravagent individuals are vulnerable to clever advertising promotion and smooth-talking, aggressive salespersons.

To illustrate the financial burden of a homeowner that has extensive financial obligations, assume that a family has a combined gross income of $2,800. Financial obligations include the following, housing expense including utility bills of $850, two autos with payments of $250 and $325, charge accounts of $450, and credit cards of $175. The total financial obligations amount to $2,050 per month. Dividing the total debts by the gross income, the family has a debt-income ratio of 73 percent, which exceeds the normal 36 percent considered safe. If the family should encounter problems requiring additional money, they will be forced into a financial situation that could result in the foreclosure on their home.

Homeowners should always try to reduce their debt-income ratio to under 50 percent. The smaller the debt-income ratio, the more positive cash flow the homeowners will have to compensate for incidental expenses. Reducing the debt-income ratio will increase the homeowner's financial security. It will enable him to compensate for unplanned expenses and assist him in establishing financial control measures. The reduction in debt-income ratio will also enable the homeowner to prevent the occurrence of conditions that could lead to extensive financial obligations.

WHAT THE HOMEOWNER SHOULD KNOW
ABOUT MORTGAGE DELINQUENCY AND COLLECTION

Mortgage delinquency is a serious problem that can be controlled effectively by using the appropriate measures. A mortgage becomes delinquent at the time it is due and not paid. The mortgage is in default when the mortgagor fails to perform under any covenant of the mortgage and the failure continues for thirty days. Contrary to most homeowners' belief, mortgage lenders are not interested in foreclosing on the property. They are in business to generate interest revenues and profits for their investors. If they have to foreclose, they lose income.

Mortgage delinquency can be very costly to the homeowner. All lenders charge a late charge for a delinquency that exceeds a specified number of days. The amount of the late charge and the number of days depend on the type of loan: whether it is a FHA-insured loan or a conventional loan. On FHA-insured loans, there is a late charge of 4 percent. The late charge on conventional loans is slightly higher. Some lenders have a policy of charging the same percentage for conventional loans. For example, if a homeowner is paying a $350 mortgage payment and becomes two months delinquent, the total amount due would be $728 ($700 for two months' delinquency plus $28 for two months' late charges). Most mortgage lenders have a standard policy of not accepting the delinquent payments if all the payments, including the late charges, are not submitted at the same time. Although this practice is common in the mortgage industry, most lenders will cooperate with the homeowners in developing a mortgage reinstatement plan if the delinquency was caused by conditions or circumstances over which the homeowner had no control. If the homeowner should be faced with a serious delinquency problem that will last for several months, he should communicate with the lender to develop a long-range mortgage reinstatement plan. Once the plan has been developed, payments should be submitted on a timely basis. They should be paid with certified funds, such as a cashier's check or a money order.

Mortgage collection procedures are different for FHA-insured loans. The lender must follow the collection policies established by HUD. The lender is allowed to charge a late charge on the seventeenth day of the month since the first day of the month is the due date, the sixteenth is the fifteenth day after the due date, and, therefore, only on the seventeenth is the payment more than fifteen days delinquent. The HUD book *Administration of Insured Mortgages* requires that lenders uses specific procedures concerning the return of partial payments. A partial payment is a payment of any amount that is less than the full amount due under the terms of the mortgage at the time the payment is submitted, including late charges. The regulation indicates that the lender shall accept any partial payment made by the homeowner under certain provisions. The partial payment may be applied in any of the following ways: (1) applied toward the homeowner's account or (2) identified with the homeowner's account and held in a trust account pending disposition.

Under the HUD regulation, if the mortgage is in default, a partial payment may be returned to the homeowner with a letter of explanation if the following conditions exist:

(1) A payment has aggregated less than 50 percent of the amount then due.
(2) The payment is less than the amount agreed to in an oral or written forebearance or reinstatement plan.
(3) The property is occupied by a rent-paying tenant, and the rentals are not being applied to the mortgage payments.
(4) Foreclosure has commenced. This is considered to be when the first action required for foreclosure under applicable law has been taken.

Foreclosure by the lender cannot start until the day after the due date of the third unpaid mortgage payment. Even if foreclosure has started, HUD regulation requires the lender to allow reinstatement of the delinquent mortgage. The homeowner must submit the entire amount of the delinquency, including late charges, foreclosure costs, attorney fees, and other expenses connected with the foreclosure action.

IMPLEMENTING CORRECTIVE MEASURES
TO CONTROL MORTGAGE DELINQUENCY

Chronic mortgage delinquency may have a detrimental impact on homeowners' credit ratings. It could result in the rejection of home rehabilitation loans that may be needed desperately to correct housing deficiencies, upgrade the house, or make major home repairs. It is, therefore, essential that the application of specific corrective measures be considered to eliminate the mortgage delinquency problem. A variety of measures can be taken to control and eliminate the conditions that cause mortgage delinquency. These measures may be interacted to maximize their impact. The control measures selected to control the delinquency problem should be commensurate with the scope and magnitude of the homeowner's specific problems and conditions.

Each homeowner may be affected by one or many kinds of problems. Their financial structures may vary according to their particular circumstances, and any corrective measures that are designed must be contingent upon and adjusted to specific conditions. Some homeowners may have financial problems that require the use of a combination of corrective measures to resolve the delinquency. However, to have a more permanent positive affect, a problem analysis must be made to ascertain the extent of the problem and what corrective measures will be most effective. In order for corrective measures to be effective in controlling mortgage delinquency, the homeowner must concentrate on the following: (1) developing a more disciplined approach in managing his financial affairs, (2) being able to adjust his life-style and prepare more realistic budgets, and (3) developing budgetary skills and living within the established financial restraints.

Controlling mortgage delinquency by using specific corrective measures can also create a state of financial solvency for the homeowner. He, however, must be capable of recognizing the conditions and situations that created his financial problems. If he cannot conceptualize those factors that caused the delinquency, when the homeowner's faced with similar situations the delinquency will reoccur. Corrective measures most often used by homeowners include: (1) assets liquidation, (2) debt consolidation, (3) obtaining temporary employment, and (4) obtaining second loans on the home.

Assets Liquidation

Mortgage delinquency can be attributed to a lack of cash flow or disposable income caused by many conditions and circumstances. The cash flow of a homeowner can generally be increased. Some homeowners do not have the financial insight to identify those areas that usually can be changed, adjusted, eliminated, and modified to increase their cash flows. The homeowner must take a realistic look at his debt-income structure to identify those assets that have existing financial obligations that can be eliminated without seriously affecting the welfare of the family. The amount and time remaining on the debts must be carefully considered in order to develop a plan to maximize the cash flow. A decision must be made to liquidate assets that will not have a serious negative impact on the homeowner's welfare.

To illustrate, assume that a homeowner has a serious mortgage delinquency problem. He is five months delinquent, but does not have enough disposable income to be put on a mortgage reinstatement plan. The mortgage payment is $450 per month. The homeowner has the following debts: two car payments, $275 and $225, $150 on a twenty-one foot boat; $120 on a motorcycle, and three charge accounts totaling $125. Available assets include the following: an IRA account with the credit union that has matured at a $2,000 value, a whole life insurance policy that has a cash value of $600 and twenty-five shares of Shurway Electronics stocks, each share with a value of $8. An assessment of the homeowner's financial structure will show that several approaches could be used to eliminate the delinquency. The house is five months delinquent, which amounts to $2,250 (5 months × $450 mortgage payment). Converting the IRA into $2,000 cash and converting half of the electronic stock to cash ($850 stock value divided by 2) result in $425 cash. The homeowner would then have $2,425, which would be more than enough to pay the delinquent mortgage payments. But here there would still be the cash flow problem that caused the delinquency. The delinquency will invariably reoccur unless plans are implemented to increase the cash flow. This could be done easily by liquidating some of the unnecessary assets. By selling the second car, the boat, and the motorcycle, the homeowner would increase his cash flow by $495, ($225 second car payment + $150 boat payment + $120 motorcycle payment). Homeowners must be willing to make sacrifices and modify their living styles to eliminate conditions that cause mortgage delinquency.

SECTION 234 OF THE NATIONAL HOUSING ACT

The Department of Housing and Urban Development (HUD) is authorized to insure lending institutions against loss in case of defaults on HUD-insured loans. HUD thus enables lenders to make loans with high loan-to-value ratios on condominiums. Section 234 of the Condominium Housing Program was enacted by Congress to assist homebuyers in purchasing affordable housing and to increase the supply of privately owned housing. Before the introduction of the Section 234 housing program, lenders were not making high loan-to-value mortgage loans. This, in effect, prevented many homebuyers from purchasing condominiums because of the high down payment required as part of the underwriting standards. The HUD Section 234 housing program caused the lenders to increase their loan-to-value mortgage loans, which reduced the amount of the down payment.

Condominiums insured by HUD are required to conform to minimum property standards. These standards are designed to prevent the dwellings from deteriorating and losing their marketability. The property standards are beneficial to homebuyers because they are able to acquire better-quality homes for virtually the same price that they would pay for homes that were not affected by quality-control standards. Many developers build homes that exceed HUD's minimum property standards. Homebuyers are subjected to HUD's home loan underwriting standards when buying a condominium under the Section 234 housing program. Normally, their total housing expense cannot exceed 35 percent of their net income and total recurring debts cannot exceed 50 percent of their net income. Total recurring expenses include housing expenses in addition to monthly bills that require more than twelve months to be paid off. In some cases, HUD will modify the percentages if there are favorable compensating factors, such as excellent credit ratings, or the homebuyers have demonstrated that they have the financial management skills to control higher debt-income ratios.

The Effects of Debt Consolidation
on Financial Structures

Debt consolidation is perhaps one of the most common financial strategies used by homeowners to solve mortgage delinquency problems. It, however, is also the most misused financial strategy. Debt consolidation can be extremely effective if it is used by homeowners with certain debt configurations. Using debt consolidation without analyzing the effects could cause a homeowner to magnify his financial problems. This technique should only be used if the homeowner's remaining debts, payments, and balances could be reduced to create a substantial cash flow. Debt consolidation is not a plan that everyone should use, especially those homeowners who have extravagant spending habits that cannot be controlled. Debt consolidation tends to have the effect of financial euphoria on extravagant spenders. They feel that because of the sudden substantial increase in disposable income created by debt consolidation, a state of financial flexibility and independence is obtained. This false illusion of financial stability lures the homeowners into buying additional material things, thereby increasing total debts to a figure that may be beyond their control. The aggregation of debts causes other financial problems, which could cause the homeowners to become delinquent with their mortgages.

The importance of debt consolidation in changing the homeowner's financial structure should not be overlooked. This strategy alone can virtually eliminate cash flow problems. The misuse of debt consolidation is what adversely affects the homeowner's ability to resolve financial problems. In essence, homeowners often use debt consolidation for the wrong purposes. There are many cases where homeowners consolidated their debts to increase their disposable income and six months later these same homeowners found themselves in a more precarious financial situation, requiring additional credit counseling to prevent a financial disaster. The debt-income ratio can be controlled, but it requires the use of the three financial Ds, I mentioned before: Diligence in adhering to budgets, Discipline to control spending habits and modifying life styles, and Dedication to develop financial management skills.

18

The Housing and Urban Development (HUD) Mortgage Assignment Program

The HUD mortgage assignment program is one that is often misunderstood by homeowners and loan service officers representing lenders with HUD-insured loans in their portfolios. The mortgage assignment program allows homeowners whose mortgages are in default due to circumstances and conditions that are beyond their control to reinstate their delinquent mortgage. According to HUD, the home mortgage assignment program was designed to give financially distressed mortgagors (homeowners) the opportunity to avoid foreclosure, thereby protecting their credit standing and preventing their homes from being sold at trustee or sheriff sales.

The mortgage assignment program assists homeowners who meet the eligibility criteria by reducing or suspending the mortgage payments for up to thirty-six months. The homeowner must prove that he has reasonable financial prospect of resuming the full mortgage payments. To reduce the mortgage payments, HUD may elect, depending on the homeowner's circumstances and conditions, to extend the mortgage for up to ten years. Each individual mortgage delinquent case is treated in accordance with its own circumstances.

To be eligible for the HUD mortgage assignment program, the homeowner must meet the following eligibility criteria: (1) The homeowner must be at least three full months delinquent with the mortgage payments. For example, if April, May, and June payments have not been made, three mortgage payments would be due after the due date of the June's mortgage payment. (2) The home must be the principal residence of the homeowner, and the homeowner must not own other property that is HUD-insured. Under certain conditions, this criteria may be waived by HUD. The conditions that may cause HUD to waive the criteria are: (1) When the home has been leased or rented and the rental income is used to pay the mortgage delinquency or to make repairs needed to maintain the property in a safe and habitable condition: When other family expenses or situations have created financial problems that are beyond the homeowner's control. (2) When the homeowner owns other property that has a HUD-insured loan where the income from the property is the homeowner's principal source of income. If the homeowner voluntarily abandoned the property for more than sixty days, waiver of the principal residence requirement is not permitted by HUD. (3) When the default has been caused by circumstances beyond the homeowner's control. The circumstances must have created financial problems that made mortgage delinquency inevitable.

The following illustrations are some examples of circumstances that are beyond the control of homebuyers: (1) loss or reduction of income due to economic conditions that caused unemployment or underemployment; (2) loss of benefits received from federal, state, Social Security, and other public assistance, annuities, support payments, and pensions and loss of income due to divorce, illness, or death; (3) uninsured damaged to the home affecting the livability of the house and necessitating costly repairs; (4) expenses related to death or illness in the homeowner's household or of family members living outside the household that contributed to the loss of income and affected the homeowner's financial capacity to make the mortgage payments; (5) unanticipated increase in payments to the mortgage escrow account to compensate for past underestimates. Many lenders increase the mortgage payments to offset the increase in property taxes or insurance. This increase, in many cases, creates financial problems for the homeowner, affecting his disposable income and resulting in mortgage delinquency and default.

A key factor that must be considered in the assignment program is that the current default is what HUD looks at in determining if the homeowner is in default due to circumstances beyond his control. A problem may arise if the homeowner's mortgage was delinquent before the circumstances occurred. For example, if a homeowner was already two months delinquent before he was laid off due to business slowdown, HUD could reject the homeowner's request for an assignment because the loss of income occurred after the delinquency and the extent of the delinquency may have adversely affected the homeowner's financial capacity to prevent the mortgage default. The lender must notify the homeowner after the mortgage is three full months in default that foreclosure is being considered. The homeowner has seven days to complete and return the HUD financial form to the lender. Upon receiving the financial form, the lender must evaluate each eligibility criterion and make a decision to request or not request HUD to accept an assignment of the homeowner's mortgage. If the lender, after determining that the homeowner meets HUD's mortgage assignment eligibility criteria, must notify the homeowner in writing that HUD would be requested to accept the assignment of the defaulted mortgage. However, if the lender decides not to request that HUD accept the assignment, the homeowner must be notified of the lender's decision and advised to appeal to HUD within fifteen days to make his own request for an assignment. The lender is prohibited from foreclosing on the homeowner until HUD has reviewed the homeowner's case and made a decision to either accept the assignment or give permission to the lender to foreclose at his discretion.

Upon request by the homeowner to HUD to accept the assignment, HUD will arrange a conference between the homeowner and HUD. It is the responsibility of the homeowner to obtain documentation of the circumstances that were beyond his control and contributed to the default. Documentation could be letters of termination from his former employer, medical reports, or letters from income sources that showed a discontinuance or reduction in income. Documentation of the circumstances cannot be overemphasized. The extent of and how the circumstances are documented can have a favorable impact on HUD. Therefore, the homeowner should document all the conditions that affect his financial capacity. If HUD accepts the mortgage assignment, HUD will then become the lender and all future payments will be paid to HUD.

The mortgage assignment concept, if modified, could be used by lenders to assist homeowners who have defaulted on their conventional mortgages. The concept would prevent many foreclosures, which deprive homeowners of their homes and damage their credit ratings.

19

The Effects of Communication between Homebuyers and Lenders

Mortgage delinquency is often adversely affected by the lack of communication between the lender and the homebuyer. In many cases, the homebuyer regards the lender as overbearing, unconscionable and uncompromising. The loan service representative frequently regards the homebuyer as a delinquent derelict or a deadbeat. Both impressions are generally erroneously conceived.

Many factors affect communications between the homebuyer and loan service representative. These factors can usually be corrected by the homebuyer and lender's loan service representative coordinating the mortgage delinquency with a HUD-certified counseling agency. The most common elements that break down homebuyer and loan servicer's communications are the following: (1) indifferent attitudes and lack of cooperation by both the homebuyer and the loan service representative, (2) lack of effective supervision of the loan service representatives, (3) homebuyers who ignore or lack understanding of mortgage note responsibilities, (4) failure of the homebuyer and loan service representative to use professional services provided by HUD-certified counseling agencies.

The lack of cooperation by both the homebuyer and the loan service representative is responsible for many foreclosures. The loan service representative often develops unrealistic repayment plans that are virtually impossible for the homeowner to implement. Many of these plans are designed in accordance with information submitted by the homeowner, who inadvertently supply information that may be only partially correct. For this reason, it is of paramount importance for the loan service representative and the homeowner to use the services of a HUD-certified counseling agency. A more practical approach could then be used to resolve the mortgage delinquency problem.

The lack of supervision of the loan service representative may also create problems that could be averted with proper supervision. A supervisor should be concerned about how the representative communicates with the homeowner. Periodic monitoring of cases and follow-up with counseling agencies will detect problems that could be corrected before ineffective and costly collection habits evolve. The supervisor should review each repayment plan that is developed by the loan service representative. This would eliminate the tenancy of the representative developing repayment plans that are not commensurate with the homeowner's financial capacity. Homeowners often deliberately make promises that are not kept. Some of these homeowners have developed the skill of manipulation. They are convincing prevaricators who mislead the loan service representatives. The loan service representative have, in these situations, not communicated effectively with the homeowner's. The representatives must use firm and diplomatic communication techniques to prevent the homeowners from using an indifferent approach to resolving their mortgage delinquency problems. By using a counseling agency, the loan service representatives can maximize the effectiveness of their collection plans. The failure of the homeowner and the loan service representative to use the services of HUD-certified counseling agencies has resulted in innumerable unnecessary foreclosures. Many of these home foreclosures could have been prevented if either the loan service representative or the homeowner had consulted a counseling agency.

HUD mandates that all HUD-insured loans be referred to HUD-certified counseling agencies for counseling. It costs the government over $18,000 for every home that is foreclosed by a lender. If a counseling agency prevented 100 foreclosures, they would save the taxpayers $1.8 million. The total effect of all HUD-certified counseling agencies on the foreclosure rate could be the saving of the government and the taxpayers millions of dollars in foreclosure expenses.

Effective communication between the homeowner and the loan service representative can be improved immensely by both coordinating their efforts and plans with counseling agencies. The counselors usually can use an objective and realistic approach in developing mortgage forebearance agreements and reinstatement plans to bring the delinquent mortgage current. The delinquent homeowner will feel more relaxed working through a counseling agency.

20

Conditions That May Cause the Mortgage to Be Accelerated by the Lender

Practically all mortgages and trust notes have an acceleration clause that allows the lenders to call the entire loan due upon the occurrence of certain conditions or events. The acceleration clause is designed to protect the interest of the lenders. If they are used indiscriminately by lenders, they prevent many prospective homebuyers from purchasing homes. The due-on-sale clause allows the lender to accelerate the note. In some cases, the lender has to show that the sale of the property jeopardizes and impairs his interest. A lender may then enforce the due-on-sale clause if it can be demonstrated that conditions are sufficient to justify the acceleration of the note. For example, Brown sells his home to White, whose credit report delineated a consistent pattern of financial irresponsibility. The credit report showed several outstanding collection accounts and two judgments. It also showed that White's debt-income ratio imposed an unreasonable financial burden on the buyer. Under these conditions, the lender has ample justification for calling the loan due.

If a homeowner attempts to sell his home on an assumption, the lender will have valid reasons to enforce the due on sale clause if the buyer is not credit-worthy. The seller may be able to retain substantial interest in the home to prove that he has maintained an economic interest worth protecting.

The lender may also accelerate the loan if the homeowner develops a consistent pattern of delinquency. The legal doctrine of "impairment of the lender's security" can be used to accelerate the loan. Most homebuyers are not aware of the implications of the acceleration provisions contained in mortgages and trust deeds. Many have also lost their homes through judiciary or nonjudiciary foreclosures because they did not understand the mechanics of the acceleration provisions.

The lender may also accelerate the loan on the basis of the "economic waste" principle. This means that if a homeowner has failed to maintain the property and it has become seriously dilapidated, the lender can enforce the acceleration clause, forcing the homeowner to pay off the entire loan. This may appear to be an unconscionable act by the lender; however, when you examine the possible results of the homeowner's neglecting to maintain the property, the validity of the economic waste principle becomes apparent. An illustration would be where Lane purchased a home in a neighborhood where the homes were well maintained. The turnover rate of homes was very low compared to that of adjacent neighborhoods. Homes in Lane's neighborhood had an average market value of $55,500. Lane allowed his home to deteriorate. His children caused physical damage that was aggravated by Lane's failure to repair the damages. The neighbors complained to the lender of the economic waste that Lane had allowed to occur to the home. The lender made many unsuccessful attempts to have Lane make the repairs to enhance the appearance of the house and correct the damage caused by his children. A recent real estate appraisal obtained by the lender revealed that the property had decreased in value due to the advance deterioration. The current market value was established at $45,500. Lane had purchased the home three years ago for $52,500. He has an existing mortgage of $47,150. An examination of these facts shows that Lane owes more than the current market value. Therefore, the lender's security has been seriously impaired. The acceleration clause could be enforced on the basis of the economic waste principle. This clause is not used very often. However, it is one that should be understood by homebuyers because of its serious implications.

Sales of residential property will invariably suffer as a result of the enforcement of the due-on-sale clause by lenders who are interested in increasing the interest revenue by increasing interest rates on loans with low interest rates. There are many cases where homebuyers have refused to complete real estate transactions because lenders threatened to enforce the due-on-sale clause. This provision of the acceleration clause is of paramount importance. It can change drastically the way homes are financed and prevent many families from qualifying to purchase homes. The higher rate of interest will cause the homebuyer's housing-expense ratio to exceed the standards. To illustrate, assume that Perkins decides to purchase a home using the cash-to-mortgage approach. The seller is asking $57,000 with $15,000 CTM. Perkins is to assume an existing 8½ percent $42,000 mortgage, with mortgage payments of $346 per month. If the lender enforces the due-on-sale clause and increases the interest to 14½ percent and Perkins agrees to accept the new higher interest rate, the new mortgage payment would be $514 per month. This constitutes a substantial increase, $168 per month. Now suppose that Perkins had a gross monthly income of $1,750 and other housing expenses were: $35 for property taxes, $20 for hazard insurance, and $20 for mortgage insurance. The total housing expense would be $599. If the lender used a 28 percent housing-expense ratio, Perkins could afford only $490 per month for housing expense. Since the total housing expense on the new loan is $599, Perkins could not qualify for the home loan under the new interest rate. The effect of the acceleration clause would result in the cancellation of the sales transaction.

The due-on-sale clause prevents many homebuyers from qualifying to purchase a home. Some sellers have filed lawsuits against lenders who enforced the due-on-sale clause. Many have been successful, while others have lost their cases, which resulted in the cancellation of impending sales. The acceleration clause is an extremely significant provision. Enforcing the clause can be supported in some cases. However, there should be guidelines and limits placed on how much a lender can increase the interest rate.

Provisions of the acceleration clause, especially the economic waste provision, should be used with more consistency. The acceleration clause protects not only the lender's interest in the homes, but other homeowners from decreasing property values caused by homeowners who deliberately and willfully neglect to maintain their homes. In comparison, the due-on-sale clause is used with much more consistency because of the lender's concern to eliminate loans with low interest rates.

21

The Use of Budgets to Improve Financial Management Skills

No business could successfully operate without a budget. In fact, many businesses that have ceased operations probably had budgetary problems that affected their production and revenues. Like a successful operating business, a homeowner must be able to use a budget to control his expenditures. Using a budget effectively means more than recording expenditures. There must be a budgetary plan of financial appropriations for anticipated expenditures as well as normal household operating expenses. Once the budget has been designed, homeowners should make a dedicated commitment to adhering to the designs of the budget. A budget can be extremely cumbersome. It, however, can also assist the homeowner to avoid financial situations that have caused financial ruin for many homeowners.

Most homeowners have some kind of a budget. Some are more formalized; others mean little more than mentally keeping track of the financial obligations each month. The best approach for developing an effective budget is to adopt a formalized budget, listing income from all sources and all monthly debts, due dates, and amounts paid on each debt. The budget should be broken down in sections. Two distinct budget classifications should be used, including variable expenses and fixed expenses. Household variable expenses changes from month to month. They include traveling, other recreation, food, and utilities. These expenses usually can be controlled by the homeowner. They are generally the expenses that can be modified and easily adjusted. For example, utilities can be minimized by the homeowner using energy savings measures, such as monitoring the thermostat to control the excessive consumption of energy. Recreation is also an area that can be adjusted. This implies that the homeowner must adjust his living style and become more frugal with household expenditures and the acquisition of material things.

The budget should include two columns for expenses. One of the columns should be designated for the amount of money that is appropriated for certain variable expenses. The other column should be used for the actual amount spent during the month or budgetary period. By comparing the planned expense column with the actual expense column, the homeowner can detect any budget variances that may occur. The homebuyer may be overspending in certain areas. After analyzing the budget variances, corrective measures can be designed and implemented to bring the financial problem under control. Budget variances are unplanned expenses that exceed the amount of money appropriate for a specified expense. In some cases, budget variances denote that the amount of money appropriated for certain expenses may be unrealistic and require budget adjustments. For example, Ryder has three children. He appropriated $110 per month for food expense. After adding up the money that was spent for food, he found that the actual expense was $220. The budget variance was caused by Ryder appropriating an unrealistic amount for food expense. The expense must be adjusted to reflect a true figure for food appropriation. Other variable expenses should be analyzed for excessive spending.

Fixed expenses, once established, cannot be controlled by the homeowner. Examples of fixed expenses are mortgage payments, auto payments, insurance payments, and monthly installment accounts. Fixed expenses should be prioritized by the homeowner. Those expenses that will have the greatest impact on the homeowner's living conditions should receive top priority. Financial problems occur and are aggravated when homeowners apply funds to the wrong expenses. When this situation occurs, the effectiveness of the budget in establishing financial controls is seriously affected. Many of these homeowners who place priority on the wrong expenses use the "Rob Peter to pay Paul principle." They use money intended for a high prioritized expense to pay a less prioritized expense. For example, Lucy owns a home with a mortgage payment of $350 per month. She purchased a new car six months ago with payments of $385 per month. She took a vacation and used the mortgage money to finance the expense of the vacation. The mortgage became delinquent as a result of this misapplication of money to a less prioritized expense.

Financial forecasting should be incorporated into the budget. This includes planning for future expenditures. Lucy could have avoided the mortgage delinquency had she appropriated money for the vacation in the budget. Because of inadequate budget planning and the improper prioritizing of expenses, Lucy could lose her home through foreclosure.

There are several factors that cause major budget variances and must be considered by the homeowner. These factors, if not compensated for, could create conditions that may cause irreparable financial damage. The modification of living style is probably the most difficult adjustment to make, yet is the one of the expenses in which the greatest adjustments and savings can be made to control budget variances. Once an individual becomes accustomed to a certain living style, it is difficult to develop and adhere to budgetary designs that cause major changes in the homeowner's pattern of living. Household variable and fixed expenses can be reduced, eliminated, and prevented by the homeowner making significant modification to his living style. Using one car instead of two could reduce both fixed and variable expense. Other changes could also be made to increase the homeowner's cash flow.

Impulse buying causes variable and fixed expense to increase. Some homeowners are compulsive spenders. They buy household goods without making financial plans. These unplanned purchases cause budget variances that can be controlled by using a properly designed budget. Unplanned purchases cause a decrease in disposable income and affect the homeowner's ability to maintain effective budgetary controls.

The checking account is one of the most effective budget control tools that can be used by a homeowner. The homeowner can keep track and maintain surveillance of expenses. Checking accounts provide the homeowner with a written record of expenses that can be evaluated at the end of the planned budgetary period. Any spending variances can be easily detected and corrective measures implemented to bring them under control. A well-designed budget is meaningless unless the homeowner changes his living style and make a concerted effort to follow the budgetary designs. A budget can also assist the homeowner to eliminate financial problems and maintain controls over expenditures.

22

How to Purchase a
Government-acquired Home

The U.S. Department of Housing and Urban Development sells homes that they have acquired from homebuyers who have defaulted on HUD-insured loans. These homes are located in various neighborhoods and can be purchased through any licensed real estate broker who is on FHA's list to sell their acquired properties. Federal Housing Association (FHA)-acquired homes are sold through the bid process. Therefore, one house listed at a reasonable beginning bid price and located in a desirable neighborhood could conceivably cost the successful bidder more than its fair market value. These homes create competitive bidding because of neighborhood amenities such as prestigious locations, quality schools, and other desirable conditions. Before bidding on FHA-acquired homes, the buyer should make an assessment of the neighborhoods. If he decides to bid on a particular home, he should check the prices of similar houses in the neighborhood. At least three houses should be compared. This can easily be done by checking the homes that are listed for sale. In fact, any broker that has homes listed for sale in the neighborhood would show the home to a prospective buyer. With the information obtained from real estate sales agents about the homes in the neighborhood, the buyer will have important data to use as a basis for bidding.

The FHA bidding process should be clearly understood by real estate brokers who are submitting bids for homebuyers. One mistake could cause the bid to be rejected. FHA encourages the buyers to use a licensed participating real estate broker to submit their bids. The bid process changes on a constant basis. Brokers are aware of these changes. Therefore, all of the necessary forms can be prepared and submitted with very good chances that they will be accepted by the FHA.

There are two ways to purchase FHA-acquired homes. One way is to borrow money from a lender and use the loan to purchase the home from FHA. If the buyer meets the FHA home loan underwriting standards, the FHA will insure the loan. The FHA actually does not loan the money to the buyer, but insures the lender against a loss in case the buyer defaults on the loan. When this occurs the FHA has to pay the total amount due on the loan.

The method for computing the down payment on FHA-acquired homes changes from time to time. It is, therefore, essential for the real estate brokers to be knowledgeable about FHA sales procedures. The homebuyer's bid could be rejected if the broker fails to include all the pertinent FHA-required information on the bid form. The amount of the down payment on FHA insured loans is determined by the following formula: 03 percent of first $25,000 plus 5 percent of remaining amount, plus 10 percent of amount bid above the listing price. To illustrate, assume that the FHA has an acquired home for sale with a list price of $42,500. Using the above formula, the down payment can be determined easily. The following down payment schedule shows the amounts calculated at each step of the formula.

Down Payment Schedule

Listing Price	Computation	Down Payment Amount
$42,500	(.05 × $42,500 Listing Price)	$2,125
Amount of Bid		
$43,800		$ 130
	(.10 × $1,300 Bid Amount Above)	$1,755
	Listing Price	
	Total Amount of Down Payment	$2,255

FHA-financed sales are those sales where the FHA insures the loan against default on behalf of the lender. This, in essence, implies that should the buyer default on the loan, the FHA will pay the lender, who will then transfer title to the property to the FHA. If the buyer is the highest bidder, he must select a mortgage company approved by FHA to finance the home. The mortgage company has twenty-five calendar days to submit the completed credit package to the FHA. However, it is the buyer's responsibility to make sure that the credit package is received by the FHA within twenty-five days of the date of the contract. The homebuyer could lose his earnest money if the mortgage company fails to submit the credit package on time. It is, therefore, imperative for the buyer and the real estate broker to make sure that the mortgage company has access to pertinent information that is necessary to complete all the FHA-required documents and forms.

The FHA also has many acquired homes that they sell but do not insure. These homes, in many instances, require minor to major rehabilitation. A buyer can generally obtain a very good house for a price that may be well under the house's repaired market value. Many of these homes are sold in an "as is condition," for all cash. This, in essence, implies that the homebuyer has to arrange his own financing through a lender. There are many financial institutions that the buyer can approach to arrange financing. The buyer should get a loan commitment from a lender prior to submitting a bid to purchase a home from the FHA on an all-cash basis. If the buyer should be the successful bidder and fails to procure financing, the earnest money could be retained by the HUD. The homebuyer should also arrange to get a cost estimate to ascertain the cost of rehabilitating the home. Buying a home that requires substantial rehabilitation may defeat the purpose of obtaining affordable housing.

The lender may require the homebuyer to deposit the full amount of the rehab cost in an escrow account to insure that the home will be rehabilitated totally. An alternative to placing funds in escrow would be where the homebuyer arranges interim financing of the rehabilitation work and permanent financing for the sales price and rehab cost when the rehabilitation work has been consummated. It is possible for the homebuyer to purchase a government-acquired home in an "as is condition," have it rehabilitated, and create instant substantial equity. To illustrate, assume that a homebuyer buys a home from the government for $35,000 that requires $5,000 to rehabilitate. If the home has a market value of $55,500 after it has been rehabilitated, the buyer will have created an instant $15,000 equity in the home. If the buyer purchased a similiar house in the same neighborhood that was listed by a real estate broker, it would normally take years to accumulate an equal amount of equity. It is important that the buyer be aware of the price of homes that he intends to bid on. He should get a very good cost estimate of what it would take to rehabilitate the home. If any one of the preceding elements is miscalculated, the buyer could end up paying more than the fair market value for the home.

23

Using an
Adjusted Rate Mortgage (ARM)
to Finance a Home

Home ownership is one of the most important features of the American free enterprise system. The American dream of owing a home, however, is rapidly becoming extinct for millions of Americans. This same free enterprise system that so much pride and emphasis have been placed on is now working against certain homebuyers that fall within specific income limits. For every 1 percent increase in the interest rate, thousands of Americans are deprived of the opportunity of owing a home. Hence, the American dream for these prospective homebuyers has become wishful thinking.

The mortgage industry, realizing the diminishing supply of homebuyers, designed a mortgage that would induce lenders to make home loans available to prospective homebuyers without being locked into low-yielding fixed-rate loans. In effect, this enables the lenders to attract more investors, thereby increasing the supply of mortgage money. As the supply of money increases, so does the opportunity to buy a home at affordable rates. The Adjusted Rate Mortgage (ARM) is an instrument in which the interest rate is initially two to three percentage points below the market interest rate. The interesting feature and the key element that makes the ARM works is that the interest rate is tied into a floating index and adjusted at periodic intervals, such as one, two, or three years. This concept increases the affordability of homes and allow homebuyers to meet the home loan underwriting standards with a lower income than would be required at market rate interest. The index used varies from lender to lender. However, many lenders use a regional index, while others use treasury notes, because they reflect more realistic changes in the economy. In addition, the lender adds a margin to the index to arrive at the new interest rate. The margin is established by the lender to assure a specific return on his investment. For example, if the index is 13½ percent at the time of the adjustment and the lender has a 1 percent margin, the new interest rate would be 14½ percent. The purpose of the ARM is to enable the homebuyer to meet the home loan underwriting standards with an income that is lower than the amount that would be required at the market interest rate and to increase the lender's yield on the investment.

To illustrate the advantage of an Adjusted Rate Mortgage, assume that a homebuyer buys a $75,000 home and pays $7,500 for a down payment. The amount the homebuyer would have to finance is $67,500. The monthly mortgage payment on a thirty-year, 14 percent fixed-rate mortgage is $800. Assuming the property tax and insurance are $75 per month, the total mortgage payment, plus principal interest, taxes, and insurance (PITI), would be $875. Mortgage lenders place a limit on the amount of money that the homebuyers can afford to pay for housing. This amount is reflected as a percentage of the homebuyer's gross monthly income and is referred to as the Affordability Income Percentage (AIP). It is also often referred to as the Housing Expense Ratio (HER). The HER varies from lender to lender, with the most common range being 25 to 28 percent. The HER may be exceeded in exceptional cases where favorable compensating factors exist. Most lenders will adhere rigidly to the housing expense ratio. They realize increasing the Housing Expense Ratio would virtually program the homebuyer for mortgage default and eventually foreclosure. The purpose of the HER is to build a default safety measure that, in effect, reduces the chance of the homeowner defaulting on the home loan and losing the home through foreclosure. High Housing Expense Ratios should be avoided by homebuyers. They are the major cause of mortgage delinquency.

The homebuyer initially enjoys the benefits of a reduced mortgage payment when compared to standard fixed-rate mortgages. The payment may, however, be substantially increased or decreased after change in index is applied to the mortgage payment. The interest rate adjustment period is the time when the payment is changed to reflect changes that occurred in the index. This period may be for one, two, or three years. It is imperative that the homebuyer understand the financial impact that the ARM can have on financial status. Although the ARM enhances the homebuyer's financial situation, it can also be a financial detriment. If the homebuyer's income does not proportionately change to be commensurate with the increase in the index, the financial ability to maintain the mortgage in a current state will be jeopardized. The ARM improves the homebuyer's chances of meeting the home loan underwriting standard by reducing the amount of income required to qualify for a mortgage. The following chart depicts the amount of income required under the ARM compared with standard fixed-rate mortgages:

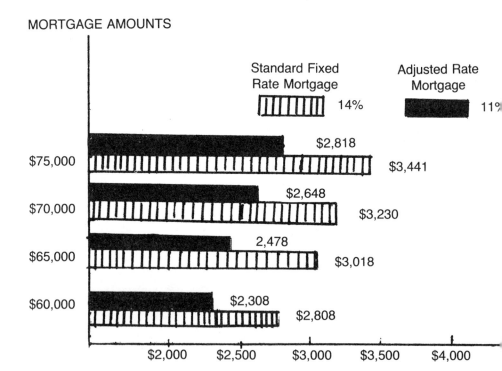

MORTGAGE AMOUNTS

Standard Fixed Rate Mortgage ▦ 14%

Adjusted Rate Mortgage ▬ 11%

$75,000 — $2,818 / $3,441

$70,000 — $2,648 / $3,230

$65,000 — 2,478 / $3,018

$60,000 — $2,308 / $2,808

$2,000 $2,500 $3,000 $3,500 $4,000

Monthly income required at various mortgage amounts. Property tax and insurance is assumed to be $75.00 per month.

The above comparison graph shows the differences in income required for various mortgage amounts. For a $65,000 standard fixed rate mortgage, the homebuyer needs $3,018 per month, as compared to $2,478 per month for an Adjusted Rate Mortgage. The homebuyer needs $540 more per month to qualify for the same mortgage amount using the Standard Fixed-Rate Mortgage. This means that the homebuyer must increase his income by 22 percent in order to meet the housing expense ratio for the same mortgage amount.

One of the major disadvantages of the ARM is that although the initial rate may make the home affordable, the subsequent increases in the mortgage interest rate could create dire financial problems for the homebuyer. This usually occurs when the homebuyer fails to make an accurate and realistic assessment of his projected income. If the homebuyer is employed in a business where salary increases are on an infrequent basis or at insignificant amounts, the income could conceivably lag behind the increases in mortgage payment. If this condition should continue, the homeowner may be faced with the dilemma of selling the home or losing it through foreclosure.

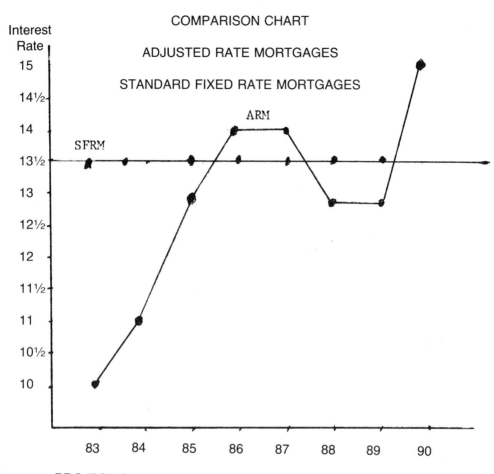

COMPARISON CHART

ADJUSTED RATE MORTGAGES

STANDARD FIXED RATE MORTGAGES

PROJECTION OF DECREASES AND INCREASES IN INTEREST OVER
EIGHT YEARS

The above graph delineates what could happen to interest rates over a projected period of time. The graph shows how Standard Fixed Rate Mortgages (SFRM) compare with Adjusted Rate Mortgages (ARM). The ARM can over a period of years exceed SFRM interest rates. This increase or decrease in ARM's interest rate will cause the mortgage payments to change accordingly. It is essential for the home-buyer to make a realistic assessment of his financial capacity to determine if there will be ample income to compensate for drastic increases in interest rates.

The advantage of the ARM is that a significant lower rate can be obtained upon purchasing the home. Notice that in 1983 the ARM interest rate is 10 percent while the SFRM is 13½ percent. However, if the economy causes the ARM to increase as depicted in the graph, the mortgage payment would be increased significantly. In 1990, the ARM increased to 15 percent, 1½ percent above the SFRM. This change in interest rate could cause a drastic change in mortgage payment.

One of the most devastating things about ARM is the MPSA (Mortgage Payment Shock Affect). This affect occurs when the interest rate increases to reflect the change in index after the initial mortgage payment has been reduced substantially below the market interest rate. ARMs that do not have annual interest caps or monthly payment caps can put the homebuyer in an extremely precarious financial condition. This condition is created when the homebuyer purchases a home using a substantial interest discount or buy-down that is far below the initial market rate. To illustrate, assume that the initial market interest rate is 13½ percent. The homebuyer purchased the home with a 5 percent interest discount reduced to 8½ percent. If the selling price of the home was $75,500 and the buyer paid $7,500 as a down payment, the amount of the mortgage would be $68,000, ($75,500 less $7,500 down payment). This amount would be financed at 8½ percent for thirty years to determine the mortgage payment the first year. The mortgage payment for the first year would be $523. If the index for the adjustment period is 14½ percent and the lender's margin is 1½ percent, the new rate would change to 16 percent after the first index adjustment change. The mortgage payment would increase to approximately $908, assuming that the principal balance of the mortgage was reduced slightly by the previous year's mortgage payments. The interest rate of 16 percent would constitute a staggering increase in the monthly mortgage payments of $385. This represents a 74 percent increase in the mortgage payments, which could have a detrimental impact on the homebuyer's ability to maintain the mortgage in a current state. Because of the MPSA, private mortgage insurance companies are refraining from insuring loans that have substantial interest discounts. HUD is also modifying its standards on ARMs because of the higher risks to the homebuyers that lead to mortgage delinquency and, in many cases, mortgage default. In order to get private mortgage insurance, lenders will be forced to modify their ARMs to eliminate or alleviate the MPSA. Homebuyers can protect themselves by obtaining ARMs that have interest caps on the life of the mortgage as well as annual interest caps. ARMs that have monthly payments caps and annual interest caps would virtually eliminate the MPSA, which has been responsible for many homeowners losing their homes because the mortgage payments increased beyond their financial limitations.

An innovative feature that would protect the homeowner involves having the interest rate remain stable for three or five years. This period of time would allow the homebuyer time to make necessary financial adjustments for interest rate fluctuations.

Homebuyers should be extremely alert when using an ARM to finance a home. Selecting an ARM that is not commensurate with the financial limitations of the homebuyer could lead to mortgage delinquency, default, and eventually foreclosure. Monthly payment caps may create a condition where the mortgage payment is less than the monthly interest expense on the loan. When this condition occurs, the mortgage principal balance increases. This condition is referred to as negative amortization. It is a condition that occurs when the ARM incorporates monthly payment caps that are designed to protect the homebuyers against substantial increases in the mortgage payment and previously referred to as Mortgage Payment Shock Affect (MPSA). Lenders often refer to negative amortization as deferred interest or catch-up payments. Regardless of how negative amortization is labeled, the effect is the same: the mortgage payment is not large enough to cover the interest expense.

To illustrate the effect of negative amortization, assume that a homebuyer purchased a $70,000 home, with an initial ARM interest rate of 12 percent. The buyer pays $5,000 as a down payment. Assume that the index changed to 12½ percent and the lender established a 2 percent margin. The initial mortgage payment on $65,000 ($70,000 sales price of home less $5,000 down payment) is $669 per month. If the ARM has a mortgage payment cap of 7½ percent, the mortgage payment after the first adjustment period with the 7½ percent cap would be $719 per month ($669 initial mortgage payment + $50 mortgage payment cap at 7½ percent). The new mortgage interest rate is 14½ percent (12½ percent new index + 2 percent lender margin). The new payment would be approximately $795 per month. The difference between the $719 mortgage payments with the 7½ percent monthly cap and $795 new mortgage payment at 14½ percent interest is $76. This figure represents the amount of the monthly negative amortization that must be added to the principal balance of the loan. The amount of the annual negative amortization is $12 \times \$76 = \$912$. It is obvious that mortgage monthly payment caps can prevent Mortgage Payment Shock Affect. However, the homebuyer is faced with a growing mortgage in which he owes more than he borrowed to purchase the home.

The homebuyer can also obtain protection from the MPSA by selecting an Adjusted Rate Mortgage that has a cap on how much the interest can increase during the adjustment period. The interest cap prevents the mortgage payments from exceeding the homebuyer's income capacity. The interest caps provide a safety measure against an overheated economy where the inflation and other economic factors have caused the interest rate to substantially increase. The following schedule shows the financial effects that adjusted-rate mortgages with and without interest caps can have on a homebuyer's financial status. The statistical information is based on an Adjusted Rate Mortgage that has an initial interest rate of 12 percent and amortized over thirty years. Assume that the interest rate increases 2½ percent the second year and 3 percent the third year.

Adjusted Rate Mortgage Comparison Schedule

Year	Interest Rate	ARM with Interest Cap	Percent Increase	Interest Rate	ARM without Interest Cap
1	12%	$669	0	12%	$669
2	14%	$769	19%	14½%	$794
3	16%	$870	42%	17½%	$948

The schedule shows that the mortgage payment increased from $669 the first year to $769 with the 2 percent interest cap. This represents a 15 percent increase in the mortgage payment. Without the interest cap, the mortgage payment increased by $125, which is a 19 percent increase in the mortgage payment. During the third year, the mortgage payment without the interest cap increased by $279 ($948 mortgage payment without interest cap less $669 initial mortgage payment). This represents a drastic 42 percent increase in the mortgage payment. If the homebuyer lacks financial skills to maintain budgetary control, the increase in mortgage payment could result in mortgage default and foreclosure. Monthly payment caps, however, do not prevent negative amortization from occurring. At some point in time, the negative amortization will reach a limit at which the lenders will require that the homebuyers commence making mortgage payments to completely amortize the mortgage. The homebuyer should be aware of the amount of negative amortization that may occur on the mortgage before he is required to make payment to amortize the amount that has accumulated. This knowledge will enable the homebuyer to make provisions and fiscal plans to pay the additional interest expense incurred as a result of the negative amortization. Knowledge of the various effects of the ARM will help the homebuyer to select features that will make the mortgage more affordable.

ARMS WITH INTEREST RATE CEILING CAPS
OVER THE LIFE OF THE MORTGAGE

The homebuyers can create additional protection against high interest rates by insisting on the lender incorporating an interest rate cap on the life of the mortgage. This assures the homebuyer that no matter how high the interest rate goes, the maximum interest that would be charged is limited by the amount specified in the mortgage. Assume that a homebuyer purchased a $75,000 home in which a $10,000 down payment was made. The mortgage amount to be financed is $65,000. The homebuyer financed the home with a thirty-year Adjusted Rate Mortgage with an initial interest rate of 12 percent. Assume that the ARM has a 2 percent annual interest cap and a 5 percent cap on the interest rate that covers the life of the mortgage. The interest rate increases 2½ percent the second year, 2½ percent the third year, and 1 percent the fourth year. These interest caps will protect the homebuyer against the Mortgage Payment Shock Affect, where the interest rates substantially increase the first few years. Without the protection offered by interest caps, homebuyers may be confronted with rapidly increasing mortgage payments that could conceivably exceed their financial limitations. The following schedule compares the ARM with an annual interest rate cap and a 5 percent interest rate cap over the life of the mortgage.

Five Percent Interest Rate Cap over the Life of the Mortgage

Year	Interest Rate	ARM Mortgage Payment with Cap	Interest Rate	ARM Mortgage Payment without Life Cap
1	12%	$669	12%	$669
2	14%	$769	14½	$794
3	16%	$870	17%	$923
4	17%	$922	18%	$975

The schedule shows that regardless of the amount of the annual increase in the interest rate, the annual interest cap prevents the mortgage payment from increasing beyond the homebuyer's financial capacity. The interest cap on the life of the mortgage places a restriction on how much the interest can increase. In the preceding example, the maximum amount of interest the lender can charge is 5 percent and the interest rate over the life of the mortgage cannot exceed 17 percent.

Ceiling caps on the interest rates are invariably the most effective form of protection against the financial impact of spiraling interest rates. But as disclosed in a previous section, negative amortization evolves from monthly mortgage payment caps. Negative amortization that occurs from monthly payments caps is not as bad as many homebuyers conceive it to be. If the ARM has a limit on how much the negative amortization can increase and a payment schedule that is designed to pay the accrued interest without substantially increasing the mortgage payments, there would be no adverse financial impact on the homebuyer. To prevent negative amortization from accumulating to a point where it would cause a substantial and drastic increase in mortgage payments, the ARM should contain features that would extend the payments out over a longer period of time to effectively pay off the accumulated interest without imposing a financial burden on the homebuyer—for example, a restriction that prohibits the interest from increasing to a level that would require more than a 15 percent increase in mortgage payments to eliminate the negative amortization over a specified period of time.

THE EFFECT OF ADJUSTED RATE MORTGAGES ON FISCAL AND BUDGETARY PLANS

An Adjusted Rate Mortgage without a mortgage payment or interest rate cap can wreck a homebuyer's fiscal and budgetary controls and plans. It is therefore of paramount importance for the homebuyer to make a realistic assessment of his projected income to enable him to evaluate his financial capacity to make future mortgage payments. Many homeowners have lost their homes because of substantial increases in the ARM's mortgage payments. To illustrate the financial impact of Adjusted Rate Mortgage without safety measures to prevent the rapid increase in mortgage payments, assume that Taylor purchased a home using a thirty-year Adjusted Rate Mortgage with an initial interest rate of 9 percent. The ARM did not have any type of interest or mortgage payment caps. Assume that the interest increased 3 percent the second year and 2½ percent the third year. The house sold for $75,000. Taylor paid $10,000 down and obtained a $65,000 ARM. The property tax and insurance are assumed to be seventy-five dollars per month. The total mortgage payment is $598 ($523 mortgage payment at 9 percent for 30 years + $75 property tax and insurance). The lender requires that the housing expense must not exceed 28 percent of gross monthly income. Taylor has a monthly income of $2,300 per month; therefore, .28 × $2,300 = $644. Since the housing expense of $598 does not exceed 28 percent of Taylor's gross monthly income, he qualified for the loan. Assume that Taylor's salary increase 3 percent for the second and third year after he purchased the home. The following schedule shows the financial impact that an Adjusted Rate Mortgage without mortgage payment or interest caps can have on the homebuyer fiscal and budgetary plans.

Interest Caps and Salary Increase Schedule

Year	Interest Rate	Mortgage Payment	Gross Monthly Income	Salary Increase	Change in Mortgage Payment
1	9%	$598	$2,300	0	0
2	12%	$742	$2,369	$69	$144
3	14½%	$866	$2,440	$71	$124

The schedule shows that Taylor's wage increased only by $69 per month while his housing expense increased by $144 the second year after he purchased the home. This type of increase could have a serious and detrimental impact on Taylor's budget. Monthly payments caps would have prevented the substantial increase in the mortgage payments. They would have caused the mortgage payment to remain within Taylor's financial limitations.

A homebuyer considering financing a home with an Adjusted Rate Mortgage should obtain knowledge of the various features. This will assist the homebuyer in selecting an ARM mortgage that has features that are commensurate with his financial status. He will be able to implement fiscal and budgetary measures to compensate for the fluctations of the mortgage payments. Adjusted Rate Mortgages are not for every homebuyer. ARMs can be effective mortgage instruments for some homebuyers; however, they can also cause financial disaster for others.

It has been estimated that more than 60 percent of all mortgages used to finance homes are ARMs. This increase may be attributed to the increase in the cost of buying a home. This trend of using ARMs to finance homes appear to be increasing in all sections of the country. ARMs have made home ownership affordable for millions of prospective homebuyers. They, however, present a higher risk to lenders. The higher risk and the increasing incidence of foreclosure on homes financed with ARMs have caused the HUD and private insurance firms to tighten their policies for insuring ARMs.

Homebuyers should be concerned about various provisions of the mortgage. They should not use the ARM to purchase a home whose mortgage payments will be beyond their financial capacity after the first few interest adjustment periods. Many homebuyers use the ARM to buy a larger home with attractive amenities only to find that, two or three years later, they cannot maintain the mortgage payments. The best and most important advice and information for the homebuyer is to evaluate the various features of the ARMs and select an ARM that the anticipated income can support.

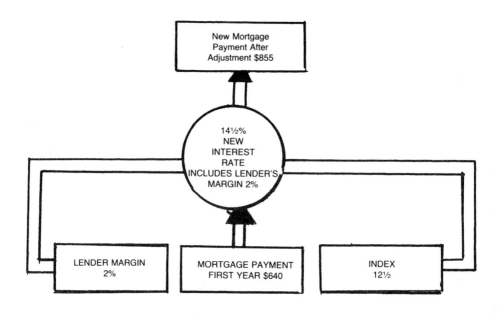

The above graphical illustration is based on a $70,000 Adjusted Rage Mortgage with an initial 10½ percent interest rate. The mortgage payment the first year is $640. The new mortgage payment will reflect a change in the index. Assume that the index change to 12½ percent. By adding the lender's margin to the new index, the new interest rate would be 14½ percent (New Index 12½% + 2% Lender's Margin). The new mortgage payment after the adjustment would be $855. This is computed by using the 14½ percent interest rate to calculate the mortgage payment. The loan is now one year old and has to be computed on the remaining mortgage balance of $69,650 for twenty-nine years.

EFFECTS OF CHANGE IN INDEX ON MORTGAGE PAYMENTS

MORTGAGE LOAN AMOUNT (The Amount to Be Borrowed)	$60,500 AMOUNT TO BE FINANCED
LENDER'S SPREAD OR MARGIN	1½ PERCENT AMOUNT ADDED TO NEW INDEX BY LENDER TO DETERMINE RATE
TERM OF MORTGAGE LOAN (Determines the Amount of Mortgage Payments)	LOAN TO BE AMORTIZED OVER 30 YEARS
INITIAL INTEREST RATE ON MORTGAGE LOAN	RATE OF INTEREST ESTABLISHED AT 11½ FOR 30 YEARS MORTGAGE PAYMENTS $599
INDEX CHANGE (Tied to One Year Treasury Bills)	ASSUME THAT THE CONDITIONS OF THE ECONOMY CAUSE THE INDEX TO CHANGE TO 13%

NEW INTEREST RATE AFTER THE FIRST CHANGE IN INDEX OR ADJUSTMENT PERIOD
SYMBOLS: New Interest Rate = NIR   Index Change = IC   Lender Margin = LM
NIR = 13% + 1½%   NIR = 14½%

NEW MORTGAGE PAYMENT
Computed on the decreased mortgage balance of $60,258 for 29 years.
New Mortgage Payment $739

24

The Balloon Mortgage and Its Effects

The balloon mortgage has been around for more than a hundred years. In fact, it has often been used on a consistent basis by those homebuyers that could not qualify for traditional and institutional financing. Balloon mortgages were used consistently in the private sector by homeowners who sold their own property. The competition in the mortgage banking industry has institutionalized balloon mortgages. Savings and loan associations, mortgage companies, and even banks are now using balloon mortgages on an increasing basis. These financial institutions, however, do not use the term "balloon mortgage." They use many sophisticated names to eliminate negative financial connotations. Some of the names used in place of balloon mortgage are: interest only loans and deferred mortgages. Regardless of the name, the effects are similar. Most homebuyers are apprehensive of balloon mortgages because of the adverse information that has been disseminated by homebuyers who lost their homes because of inability to refinance the balloon mortgage.

The balloon mortgage is an instrument in which the loan amount is amortized over an extended period of time, such as thirty years. The entire principal balance may be due in five or ten years. Interest only payments is one of the essential features of the balloon mortgage. The borrower pays only monthly interest charges for a fixed term. Upon the termination of the term, the principle balance is due. On an interest only mortgage, nothing is applied to the principal balance. To illustrate the concept of a balloon mortgage, assume that a homebuyer buys a home for $55,500 and pays $5,500 down. The homebuyer obtains an interest only 12½ percent mortgage amortized over thirty years, but due in seven years. The monthly interest would be $520. At the end of seven years, the homebuyer would still owe $50,000, the original amount financed. The balloon mortgage is widely used in the private sector, where the homebuyer, because of credit deficiencies, inadequate income, or employment stability, cannot obtain financing from institutional lenders. There are several advantages to using the balloon mortgage to finance a home.

With the balloon mortgage, the homebuyer has an opportunity to purchase a home that could not have been bought using other mortgage instruments. The balloon mortgage also gives the buyers ample time to correct the deficiencies that caused them to be rejected for a traditional mortgage. Credit deficiencies can be improved immensely. If there were collection accounts, slow credit, and a bankruptcy on the credit report, they would all be removed because of the statutory period of limitations. The homebuyer also may develop action plans to improve his credit rating. If the homebuyer has unstable employment or inadequate income, he may seek job training to enable him to obtain a higher-paying job. An increase in income would improve the homeowner's opportunity of refinancing the balloon when it comes due. Another essential advantage is that the house will increase in value, giving the homebuyer equity that he would not have been able to accumulate had the balloon mortgage not been used to finance the home. Assume that the home increased in value by $15,000. The home would have a market value of $70,500, with a mortgage balance of $50,000. The homebuyer would have $20,500 equity in the home that could not have been created by renting. This equity can be used as leverage to refinance the home at the termination of the balloon mortgage. The homebuyer will also have tax advantages that would not be available to tenants. Interest and property taxes can be used to reduce his taxable income.

The balloon mortgage also has some disadvantages. One of the major disadvantages is that the homebuyer may encounter financial difficulties that may prevent him from refinancing the home. It is therefore, important for him to make careful financial plans so that he will have the credit and income capacity to refinance the balloon mortgage. The homebuyer does have the option of selling the property in the event he cannot refinance. A second disadvantage of the balloon mortgage is that most are written for a short period of time, which could affect the buyer's financial capacity to refinance the loan.

Features of the balloon mortgage can often be combined with those of other mortgages to maximize the impact in assisting homebuyers to qualify for home loans. Many major developers use the balloon mortgage in combination with other mortgages to reduce the amount of income required by lenders' home loan underwriting standards. To show how features of the balloon mortgage can be combined with other types of mortgages, a sample of one of American's largest builder's real estate financing instrument is used as an illustration. The builder uses several mortgage concepts to design one instrument that, in effect, lowers the interest rate and reduces the amount of the down payment that would normally be required. The builder uses a 3-2-1 interest buy-down plan to decrease the monthly mortgage payments to an affordable level. The buyer pays interest only during the interest buy-down period. This is a feature of the balloon mortgage that allows the buyer to postpone a part of the selling price of the home until a specified date. The builder also buys the mortgage interest down 1 percent for the life of the loan. The 1 percent buy-down is an element found in the Pledge Account Mortgage (PAM), where a sum of money is deposited to a special account that is used to reduce the interest. At the end of twenty years, the mortgage is adjusted to the prevailing rate, and it remains constant for the duration of the loan. In effect, this adjustment period is similar to that of the Renegotiable Mortgage (REM) or the Rollover Mortgage (ROM), where the interest is changed at predetermined intervals. Two mortgage notes are used to reduce the down payment, which, in essence, is equivalent to having a second mortgage on the home. Although the buyer pays one mortgage payment, the payment covers two notes. The following schedule shows how the builder used features of various mortgages to design one security instrument that would have multiple effects in reducing the interest rate and the down payment.

Features of Builder's Innovative Mortgage Instrument

Mortgage	Mortgage Feature	Mortage Effect
Balloon Mortgage	Interest only payment	Reduces mortgage payment
Pledge Account Mortgage	Interest reduction	Reduces mortgage payment
Second Mortgage	Two mortgage notes	Reduces down payment
Interest Buy-down	Interest reduction	Reduces mortgage payment
Renegotiable Mortgage	Reduced interest	Reduces mortgage payment

The balloon mortgage can be designed to be amortized over thirty years but due in five years. The long amortization period is the main characteristic of the Standard Fixed Rate mortgage. It, in effect, reduces the mortgage payments. Therefore, the amount of income required for a home loan is decreased. The balloon mortgage adds another financial dimension to the ways home are financed.

25

Buying a Home Using the
Blended Interest Mortgage (BIM)

Many would-be homebuyers are finding it very difficult to buy homes because the interest rates and the cost of homes make it financially impossible for them to qualify for the home loan underwriting standards. The American dream of owning a home is fast becoming an illusionary vision that may not ever be realized. Literally thousands are being forced from the housing market because of the spiraling cost of construction and the high interest rates. HUD realized that certain homebuyers falling within specific income levels would never have the opportunity of buying a home. Hence the government designed various housing programs to make housing opportunities available to these homebuyers. The Federal National Mortgage Association known as Fannie May, is currently pushing the Blended Interest Mortgage (BIM) as a financing design to circumvent high interest rates and to make more mortgage money available for homebuyers to buy homes that they could not purchase at a higher interest rate. The BIM will, in effect, provide opportunities for homebuyers to purchase existing homes at an interest rate that is slightly lower than the market rate. The BIM will also benefit the lender, because it will allow him an opportunity to decrease his portfolio of low interest rate loans.

The BIM interest rate is determined by taking the existing interest rate on the loan and blending it with the current market interest rate to come up with the new blended rate, which is lower than the market rate. This, in effect, means that the homebuyer's income can be less than what it would have to be if the home were purchased at a higher interest rate. The BIM interest rate is derived by computing the interest on the existing balance at the existing rate. The interest is then computed on the difference between the existing mortgage balance and the sales price less the down payment. The two computed interest amounts are added together and divided by the sales price to obtain the new Blended Interest Rate. The mathematical effect is a reduction in the current market rate and, consequently, lower monthly mortgage payments. To illustrate: Assume that a homebuyer purchases a home from a seller with a $30,000 mortgage balance and an interest rate of 8 percent. The sales price is $65,000 and the current market interest rate is 13 percent. The homebuyer is paying $5,000 down. The new Blended Interest Rate can be computed by using the following calculations: .08 existing interest rate × $30,000 existing mortgage balance = $2,400. This amount must be added to the amount computed by multiplying the current market interest rate by the difference between the existing mortgage, $30,000, and the sales price of $65,000 less the $5,000 down payment. [$65,000 − [$30,000 + $5,000] = $4,900. $3,900 [amount of interest at current market interest rate] + $2,400 [amount of interest on existing loan = $6,300.] The total amount of interest, $6,300, divided by the new mortgage amount, $65,000, sales price less $5,000 down payment ($6,300/$60,000) = 10.5 percent. This is the new Blended Interest Rate, which is slightly lower than the 13 percent current market interest rate. The effect of this new Blended Interest Rate on the new $60,000 mortgage compares favorably with the current market rate on the same $60,000 mortgage. The monthly mortgage payment using the Blended Interest Rate would be $549, compared with mortgage payments of $664, under the 13 percent market interest rate. The savings under the Blended Interest Rate would amount to $115 per month. In essence, the homebuyer would need less income to qualify for home loan underwriting standards. The seller could enhance the marketability of the home by using the Blended Interest Rate as a way to finance the home. The Blended Interest Rate will also allow the homebuyer to qualify for a larger mortgage amount, which also means that a larger home could be purchased. Although the BIMs are relatively new, they are becoming very popular. The homebuyer should evaluate many ways of financing a home prior to buying. The evaluations must be based on his financial circumstances to determine which financing plan will be compatible with their needs.

The Blended Interest Rate Mortgage is a financing method that will enable the homebuyer to buy a home at a smaller interest rate. The homeowner would still have to meet the lender's home loan underwriting standards. He, however, would avoid paying a high down payment that would be required normally if he purchased the home using the Cash-To-Mortgage (CTM) financing technique. The homebuyer would be required to obtained new financing. Therefore, the years remaining on the existing mortgage might be substantially less than the thirty years that would be required for new financing. For tax reduction, the Blended Interest Rate Mortgage has a significant advantage over many other mortgages, especially the Cash-To-Mortgage and some newly written Adjusted Rate Mortgages that have large interest rate reductions. The homebuyer would have more interest to deduct from his income; therefore, his disposable income would be increased. The homebuyers would have more homes to choose from, because more sellers would be willing to sell their homes because, with new financing, the seller has a better chance of getting the fair market price for his home. In many cases, especially owner's carrybacks and Cash-To-Mortgage Sales, the buyer has the leverage of negotiating a reduced sales price because of the larger amount of money that is generally required. Since the buyer is qualifying for new financing and the down payment will be lower, the fair market price of the home can be negotiated successfully.

26

Buying a Home Using the Cash-To-Mortgage (CTM) Approach

Today many homebuyers buy homes using the Cash-To-Mortgage method. This is an extremely popular way of purchasing a home. It is also the way in which thousands of homebuyers are exploited by sellers and real estate agents. Some homebuyers use their life savings or the equity they got out of a home they sold to buy an unaffordable dream home only to find several months later that the gleaming home is forcing them into financial ruin. The CTM aproach is an expedient way of buying a home. It, however, can be a nightmare for the first-time homebuyer, who has no experience in home buying, or the over-zealous buyer looking for his mansion.

There are innumerable items that should be investigated prior to buying a home using the CTM approach. First, the homebuyer should check with the lender to see if the loan is assumable. Most lenders have incorporated due-on-sales clauses in the trust notes. This, in essence, means that when the homeowner sells the home, the lender can activate the due-on-sales clause and call the loan due and payable. When this occurs, the buyer will have to refinance the home, usually at a higher rate of interest; hence the mortgage payments will be substantially increased. Assume that a seller has an outstanding mortgage of $55,500 at 10½ percent with mortgage payments of $521. The seller is asking $10,000 CTM, which means that the sales price of the home is $65,500. If the lender enforces the due-on-sales clause and requires a 10 percent down payment, ($65,500 × .10 = $6,550) with a new interest rate of 14½ percent, the new mortgage amount ($65,500 − $6,550) = $58,550. The new mortgage payment at 14½ percent on $58,550 would be $717 per month. This represents a substantial increase of $196 in the mortgage payment. The homebuyer may not have the financial capacity to meet the home loan underwriting standards, or there may be credit deficiencies that may cause the homebuyer to be rejected. Second, the homebuyer should always check the status of the mortgage. This can easily be done by checking with the lender. The homebuyer should obtain the seller's loan number in order to expedite the retrival of the loan balance and to determine if there are any delinquent mortgage payments. Some sellers have sold their homes when they were three or four months delinquent with their mortgage payments. Under these circumstances, the unsuspecting homebuyer is forced to pay the back delinquent mortgage payments to prevent foreclosure proceedings by the lender. In some cases, the delinquent mortgage payments can amount to several thousand dollars; hence it is imperative for the homebuyer to get the current status of the mortgage. Third, a title search should always be ordered, especially if the home is being purchased directly from the seller. There have been many cases where overzealous buyers have purchased homes that had delinquent second mortgages that they failed to investigate during the initial sales negotiations. The second mortgage lenders can be extremely aggressive in collecting delinquent mortgage payments. If the buyer fails to correct the delinquency on the second mortgage, the lender can foreclose and have the home sold at a trustee sale. Since the lender holding the second mortgage can bid at the trustee sale, he will purchase the home for the amount due on the second loan. The homeowner would then lose all equity he had in the property.

In inspecting a home, the homebuyer should note if any improvements have been made on the home, such as a room addition, swimming pool, room enclosure, or new roof or fireplace. This may indicate that the seller has an outstanding second mortgage and is inadvertently or deliberately failing to disclose this information to the unsuspecting buyer. The cost of a title search is infinitesimal when compared to the exorbitant expense of paying on a second mortgage that was not discovered during the sales transaction. The sales price of the home can be adjusted to compensate for the second mortgage if it is discovered. If not, the homebuyer has to live with his costly mistake or pursue costly litigation, which in many cases may not be successful. This problem could be eliminated by the buyer using a title company to process the transactions. The Cash-To-Mortgage approach to buying can be advantageous to the buyer, providing the loan is assumable. The homebuyer will enjoy the benefits of a lower rate of interest; therefore, the the mortgage payments will be significantly lower than a new mortgage. One major disadvantage of using the Cash-To-Mortgage approach is that very often the homebuyer is talked by an unscrupulous real estate sales agent into buying a home that is beyond his financial capacity. Since the sales agent's commission is determined by the price of the home, the homebuyer may be exploited if he does not have a real estate attorney to explain and negotiate terms that are to his benefit.

The Cash-To-Mortgage technique of buying a home is used most often by those homebuyers that cannot meet the home loan under-writing standards. The most common reasons why buyers cannot qual-ify for home loans are the lack of income and the existence of various credit deficiencies. These two factors also may be a problem if the seller's lender enforces the due-on-sales clause and require the buyers to obtain new financing. This could result in the buyer's being rejected by the lender.

Buying a home using the Cash-To-Mortgage method usually re-quires larger amounts of money, due to substantial equity that the seller has accumulated in the home. There are many situations where homeowners have owned their homes for only a few years with small annual increases in market values. When this condition exists, the amount of money needed for a Cash-To-Mortgage transaction will be smaller in comparison with that need to purchase homes located in a prestigious neighborhood and with modest annual increases in market value. To reduce the amount of money required to buy a home using the Cash-To-Mortgage approach, the buyer should look for sellers who have owned their homes for no more than three years. This approach will enable the buyer to decrease the money needed to purchase a home.

FLEXIBLE LOAN OPTION (FLOP)
ON THE PRINCIPAL MORTGAGE BALANCE

The Adjusted Rate Mortgages enjoyed immense popularity for several years. They became known as a panacea for replacing and reducing the number of low-interest loans that lenders were carrying on their books. In fact, in some geographical areas, over 70 percent of new mortgages loans written were ARMs. Although the ARMs became ex-tremely popular with lenders as well as homebuyers, they have caused many homebuyers to become delinquent and eventually default on their mortgages. HUD and private mortgage insurance corporations began to tighten up on the loan criteria. The foreclosure and default rate on ARMs were substantially higher than on Standard Fixed Rate Mortgages. Lenders began to modify their ARMs to reduce the chance of the homebuyer defaulting on the loan. They added monthly payment, annual interest, and lifetime ceiling caps to prevent mortgage payment shock, a condition where the increases in interest rates cause the mort-gage payments to increase to a higher amount which eventually leads to delinquency and default. These added features of the ARM gave the homebuyer a higher degree of protection against the Mortgage Payment Shock Affect. However, like an automobile when additional options are added, the mortgage becomes more costly to the homebuyers.

Resentment of ARMs led to an improved mortgage instrument that attracted homebuyers without locking the lenders into long-term low-interest–yielding loans. The Flexible Loan Option on the Principal Balance Mortgage (FLOP) is a sophisticated version of the Adjusted Rate Mortgage (ARM), with features of other widely used mortgage instruments. One of the essential features of the FLOP mortgage is that it prevents the devastating effect of mortgage payment shock. The homebuyer is able to enjoy mortgage payment stability without experiencing the financial impact of increases in the mortgage payments caused by the ARM's annual adjustments.

The FLOP mortgage is an outgrowth of several popular mortgage instruments. The purpose of the FLOP mortgage was to come up with features that would overcome many of the drawbacks found in existing mortgages, such as mortgage payment shock, in which the monthly mortgage payments substantially increased, affecting the homebuyer's financial capacity to sustain the mortgage in a current state. The entry of the FLOP mortgage into the home lending industry as a home financing method has received much attention. Many mortgage experts believe that the FLOP mortgage will be substituted for many of the existing mortgages because of the attractive inducements that are absent from other popular mortgage instruments. As previously stated, the FLOP mortgage contains features found in several mortgages that are widely used by homebuyers and the lending industry, including the Adjusted Rate Mortgage, the Rollover Mortgage, the Standard Fixed Rate Mortgage, and the interest reduction or buy-down plans offered by builders. The FLOP mortgage eliminates mortgage payment shock by using a feature found in the Rollover Mortgage. This feature is implemented by using a fixed period of time in which the mortgage payments remain constant for a specified period of time, such as five-year adjustable periods. This means that if the initial interest rate is 12 percent on a thirty-year, $65,000 mortgage, the monthly mortgage payment would be $669 and it would remain at this fixed rate for five years. At the end of five years, the homebuyer has the option of converting the principle balance of the mortgage to a twenty-five–year fixed-rate mortgage in which the mortgage payments will remain constant for the remaining life of the loan. If the interest rate substantially increases by the fifth year, the FLOP mortgage contains a feature that allows the homebuyer to roll over the mortgage for another five years. This is the principal feature of the Rollover Mortgage that is used

105

widely in Canada. The new interest rate is calculated by using the average of the four previous years and the prevailing rate on one-year ARMs.

To illustrate, assume that the current prevailing ARM interest rate is 14 percent and the interest rates for the four previous years were 12½, 15, 17, and 14 percent. The new interest rate for the next five years would be 14½ percent, computed by adding the previous four years' interest rates (12½ + 15 + 17 + 14 + 14) and dividing by five. This composite interest rate feature attracts buyers because it allows them the option of utilizing an interest rate that is lower than the current market rate, which is generally 2 percent higher than ARM's interest rates.

There are also some disadvantages of the FLOP mortgage of which the homebuyer should know. First, under the FLOP mortgage, although the homebuyer is protected against the Mortgage Payment Shock Affect because of the 5-year adjustment period, they cannot enjoy the benefits of decreased mortgage payments should the index cause a reduction in the interest rate. For example, if the initial FLOP mortgage interest rate is 14 percent and the change in index caused the interest to decrease to 12 percent, the homebuyer's mortgage payment would not decrease, but would remain constant until the end of the adjustment period. The homebuyer who used an ARM to finance the home would pay a much lower mortgage payment because of the decrease in the interest rate. It is therefore conceivable for the mortgage payment to decrease 15 to 30 percent under an ARM while there would be no change in the FLOP mortgage payment. If the index caused a substantial increase in the interest rate, there would be an opposite effect on the mortgage payment. The homebuyer's mortgage payment would increase substantially under the ARM mortgage and could eventually lead to mortgage payment shock, resulting in mortgage default and imminent foreclosure. Although the FLOP mortgage payment is based on an interest rate that is on the average 2 percent lower than market rate and remains constant until the end of the adjustment period, the index may increase each year, which could cause the interest to exceed the mortgage payment, resulting in negative amortization. This is a feature and a condition that is found in the Adjusted Rate Mortgages that have monthly payment caps. To compare the Standard Fixed Rate, ARM, and the FLOP, the following information is used to show the changes in the interest rates of the mortgages. Assume that a buyer uses a FLOP mortgage to finance a home. The initial FLOP interest rate is 12 percent and the initial market interest rate is 14 percent. During the first five-year adjustment period, the change in index caused the following sequential changes in interest

106

rates: 14 percent, 17 percent, 15 percent, and 14 percent. The prevailing ARM interest rate at the end of the fifth year is 15 percent. During the next five-year adjustment period, the index caused the following changes in the interest rates: 17 percent, 16 percent, 15 percent, and 13 percent. The market interest rate after the first five-year adjustment period was 15 percent. The following graph shows the interest rates of each of the three mortgages—Standard Fixed Rate, ARM, and FLOP.

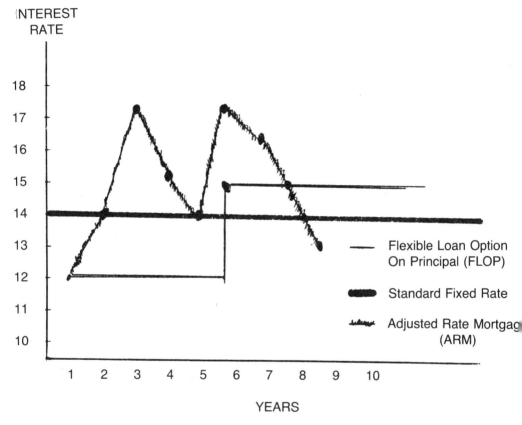

The graph shows the difference in the interest rate of the FLOP mortgage compared to the Standard Fixed Rate mortgage and the Adjusted Rate Mortgage. Under the ARM, the mortgage payments and interest rate continues to be affected by the change in index, while the interest rate remains constant under the FLOP mortgage. The graph also shows that under the ARM, the interest rate could fall below the Standard Fixed Rate mortgage. If the homebuyer averages the interest rates, the effective rate could conceivably be lower than the interest on a standard fixed rate mortgage.

107

27

The Effects of Buying a Home with a Growing Equity Mortgage (GEM)

Real estate financing has become extremely diversified. There are financing plans that can virtually meet the financial needs of most homebuyers who have reasonable debt-income ratios. The Growing Equity Mortgage (GEM) is a unique financing technique that works differently from other innovative mortgage instruments. The GEM financing plan is designed for homebuyers whose incomes increase at a moderate rate. The Growing Equity Mortgage can be construed as a high-income homebuyer's mortgage. It will cause the average worker and homebuyer dire financial problems. Unlike the typical Adjusted Rate Mortgages and Interest Reduction Mortgages, the GEM payments increase a specified percent each year for approximately twelve years, then level off and remain constant. A normal increase would be from 3 to 5 percent. The difference between the GEM and the Adjusted Rate Mortgage is that the ARM payments are adjusted to a special index that changes on a periodic basis. The change in mortgage payments involves an increase or decrease in the interest rate in which the entire amount could conceivably be applied to the interest. Under the GEM, the payments increase each year; however, the entire increase is applied to reduce the principal loan balance. The increase in the ARM payment is applied to compensate for the change in interest rate. None of the increase in payment is applied to reduce the principal loan balance; therefore, the GEM mortgage can be paid off in fifteen years, compared to the thirty years required to pay off other types of mortgages. The combination of the increase in the GEM payment where the entire increase goes toward reducing the principal loan balance and the amount required to amortize the loan causes the principal loan balance to reduce at a rapid rate. To illustrate the impact that the increase in the GEM payment has on reducing the principal loan balance, assume that a homebuyer purchased a $65,500 home and paid $5,500 for a down payment. The buyer would have to obtain a loan for $60,000 ($65,500 amount paid for the home less $5,500 down payment). Terms of the loan were for thirty years with a 14½ percent interest rate. The homebuyer purchased the home with a Growing Equity Mortgage. Assume that the GEM payments increased at the rate of 5 percent per year. The mortgage payment at 14½ percent for thirty years would be $737. The amount of the GEM increase would be $37 (5 percent × $737 monthly mortgage payment). The total amount of the GEM increase that would be applied to reduce the principal mortgage balance would be $444 (12 months × $37 dollars, amount of increase in the GEM payment). This amount is substantially more than the amount that would be applied from the regular amortization of the mortgage. The homebuyer would pay $8,832 on the principal and interest during the year ($737 monthly mortgage payments × 12 months). Approximately $132 dollars, however, would go toward reducing the loan balance, while $444, the entire amount of the GEM increase, would be used to reduce the mortgage balance. Under the developer's 3-2-1 buy-down or interest reduction plan, the mortgage payment would increase 1 percent each year for three years, while under the GEM plan the mortgage payment would normally increase at the rate 3 to 5 percent and continue to increase until the tenth or twelth year. The mortgage payment would level off and remain constant until the end of the GEM term of fifteen years. The Growing Equity Mortgage should never be considered by homebuyers whose incomes do not increase proportionately with the increase in the GEM payments. In some cases, depending on the amount of the annual increase, the Growing Equity Mortgage payments could increase as much as 50 percent in five to eight years. The GEM mortgage could cause homebuyers who do not practice financial forecasting or estimating future expenditures to default on their mortgages. Homebuyers who lack financial management skills should never finance a home with a Growing Equity Mortgage. They would be unable to compensate financially for the substantial increases in the GEM payments over an extended period of time. The homebuyers can create much more equity in the home with a Growing Equity Mortgage than they can with any other kind of mortgage.

Homebuyers who do wish to pay thirty years on a mortgage and enjoy the freedom of not paying monthly mortgage payments would benefit from using a Growing Equity Mortgage to finance their homes. The homebuyers will also be able to increase the amount of money they could borrow with a second mortgage, should it be needed for any purposes. The amount of money that a homeowner can borrow on a second mortgage is determined by the amount of equity that has been accumulated in the home. Since the equity grows substantially at a rapid rate with a Growing Equity Mortgage, the amount of money that could be borrowed would be much more than the money under other types of mortgages.

Homebuyers who fall within a certain age group and who are at the peak of their earning capacity may be in an ideal financial position to purchase a home using the Growing Equity Mortgage for financing. With proper planning, the homebuyers can finance the home with a Growing Equity Mortgage and completely pay it off by the time they retire. The GEM can assist the homebuyers to acheive a state of financial independence by releasing them from the burdens of making monthly mortgage payments at a time when their incomes have decreased.

The Growing Equity Mortgage is one of the most innovative mortgages that has been designed since the development and the implementation of home equity conversion mortgages. Like the home equity conversion mortgages, the Growing Equity Mortgage was designed to meet the housing and financial needs of a specific segment of the homebuying population. It is a real estate financial instrument that has filled a gap that was left open by lenders when they created other innovative mortgages. Mortgage lenders finally realized that there was a need for a more sophisticated mortgage instrument that would meet the demands of those homebuyers who had the financial capacity to pay off short term mortgages. One major disadvantage of the GEM is that the mortgage balance is reduced much more than in other mortgages; therefore, the homebuyer using a GEM mortgage loses some of the tax advantages through the decrease in the amount of interest that is paid on the loan.

MORTGAGE PAYMENT COMPARISON SCHEDULE

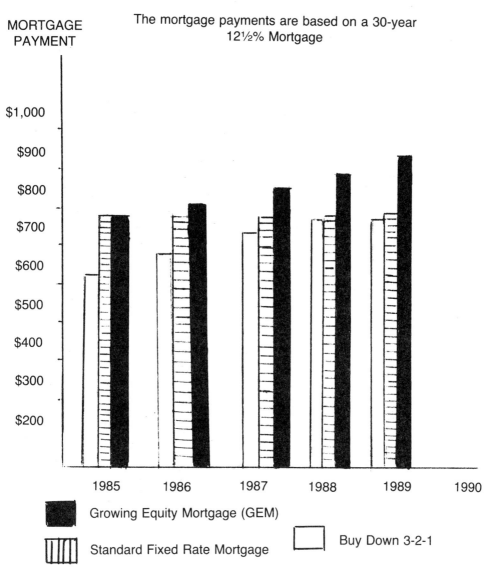

MORTGAGE PAYMENT

The mortgage payments are based on a 30-year 12½% Mortgage

■ Growing Equity Mortgage (GEM)

▥ Standard Fixed Rate Mortgage

☐ Buy Down 3-2-1

An important difference between the GEM and the Standard Fixed Rate Mortgage including the Buy Down Mortgage is that the mortgage payment under the GEM will increase continuously for a much longer time than the Buy Down Mortgage and Standard Fixed Rate Mortgage. The graph shows that the Standard Fixed Rate remains constant while the Buy Down increases and remains constant beginning the fourth year.

111

28

The Interest Reduction Plan Mortgage

The spiraling cost of home construction combined with high interest rates has virtually paralyzed the purchasing plans of thousands of homebuyers. The increase in income has not kept pace with the increase in housing cost and interest rates. Several years ago, a one income family could qualify for home loan underwriting standards. Because of the inflation factor, it now takes two incomes to qualify to purchase a home. Land developers, including the Housing and Urban Development Department, have created special mortgage instruments to encourage homebuyers to purchase homes. HUD developed the Graduated Payment Mortgage (GPM) to enable homebuyers to purchase homes that would have been virtually impossible for the homebuyer to purchase. (See chapter 40.) Land developers, in order to survive, developed many variations of the HUD Graduated Payment Mortgage. They, along with lenders, use their own names for the Buy-Down Mortgage instruments. Some commonly used names are: Buy Down Mortgages, Step Up Mortgages (SUM), and Discount Mortgages. Whatever name is used, the concept and effect are the same. The Buy Down mortgage uses a simple mathematical process where the developer places money with the lender to buy the interest down from the current market rate to a lower rate. The effect of this financing design is to enable the homebuyer to meet the home loan underwriting standards with a lower income. The following illustration of the Buy Down Mortgage shows how they work: Assume that a home developer buys the interest down 3 percent from a hypothetical 12 percent current market rate. The sale price of the home is $75,000, with a down payment of $5,000. The effect of the developer's buy-down would cause the interest rate to decrease to 9 percent. The monthly mortgage payments would be reduced substantially. After paying a $5,000 down payment and other closing costs, the homebuyer would have a $70,000 mortgage. The mortgage payment on a thirty-year 9 percent mortgage is $563. The payment on a thirty-year 12 percent mortgage is $720. Hence the homebuyer saves $157 dollars per month using the developer's Buy Down Mortgage. The various interest reduction plans have provided many homebuyers the opportunities of purchasing their first homes. Developers have been able to market their homes significantly better by using Buy Down Mortgages to attract homebuyers.

The homebuyers should check the sales prices in a subdivision where the Buy Down Mortgage is used. A few developers have sold homes in areas using Buy Down Mortgages to promote sales of slow selling homes. The developer is able to effectively use Buy Down Mortgages by obtaining high appraisals on the homes and compensating some profit. In effect, this enables the developer to buy the interest down without significantly decreasing the profit margin. The buy-down concept is tantamount to increasing the sales price to compensate for the amount of money used to lower the interest rate. To illustrate, assume that the developer buys the interest down 3 percent for three years. Using the previous illustration, the following schedule shows the amount of money that has to be deposited by the developer with the lender. After paying the closing cost and $5,000 for a down payment, the homebuyer would have a mortgage of $70,000 to finance. The approximate effect of the developer's 3-2-1 interest buy-down would be as follows:

Interest Reduction Schedule

Year	Amount of Mortgage	Interest Paid by Developer	Amount of Interest
1	$70,000	3%	$2,100
2	$69,760	2%	$1,395
3	$69,491	1%	$ 695
TOTAL INTEREST PAID BY DEVELOPER			$4,190

The above figures are approximations; actual figures may vary slightly. The $4,190 interest paid by the developer to buy the interest down is incorporated in the sales price of the home; hence the developer can buy the interest down without incurring a noticeable adverse effect on the profit margin. The Buy Down Mortgages have often been used by homebuyers whose financial status does not meet the home loan underwriting standards for the typical thirty-year fixed rate mortgage. The mortgage program should be evaluated thoroughly by the homebuyer. There are many unforseen variables that are manifested in Interest Buy Down Mortgages that could impose serious financial burdens on the homebuyers.

113

Interest reduction plans are used widely by developers. They have become the major method of financing homes in some cities. In fact, in some geographical areas, over 70 percent of all home financing is done with some form of interest reduction plan. These plans can be extremely advantageous to those homebuyers who have the necessary financial and budgetary skills to enable them to compensate for the increase in mortgage payments. They must also have incomes that will increase proportionately with the increase in monthly mortgage payment. The problem occurs when the homebuyers' income becomes stagnated or is reduced as the mortgage payment increases. Mathematically, this disparity in income and rise in mortgage payment will cause a serious financial imbalance that will eventually result in the homebuyers' defaulting on their mortgages.

Interest reduction plans do, however, allow homebuyers to purchase a larger home with a larger mortgage. The homebuyer must be alert to the consequences of buying a larger home. Reports from mortgage lenders show that the mortgage default rate for homeowners who purchased their homes with an interest reduction plan is higher than for those who used thirty-year fixed rate mortgages. In fact HUD is modifying the regulations for interest reductions plans. Some lenders are phasing out their interest reduction mortgages and encouraging homebuyers to use mortgage plans that do not create mortgage payment shock, a condition where the mortgage payment drastically increases each year and causes financial problems for the homebuyers. These interest reduction plans are designed for certain homebuyers whose incomes will increase proportionately with the increase in mortgage payments. Most of the problems occur when the seller or developer uses a substantial interest reduction and a shorter buy-down period. For example, an interest reduction plan that reduces the interest from 14½ percent to 7½ percent with an adjustment period of three years would create a mortgage payment shock, because the payments would increase over 2 percent each year.

29

The Lease Option Purchase (LOP) Arrangement

There are many homebuyers who, because of credit deficiencies, cannot meet the home loan underwriting standards. They are, therefore, unable to purchase a home. Other homebuyers have excellent credit ratings, but do not have adequate funds to pay the down payment. These prospective homebuyers have only a few options to purchase a home. The Lease Option Purchase (LOP) agreement method of financing could enable homebuyers experiencing credit and financial problems to make arrangements with the seller to buy the home at a future specified date. In the Lease Option Purchase arrangement, the seller and the buyer enter into a lease agreement where a specified sum of money is set aside out of the monthly rent to accumulate funds for the down payment. The buyer agrees to lease the home for a specified period of time under certain conditions and circumstances. The buyer has the option of purchasing the home at the end of the leasing period. If he decides not to purchase the home, the extra money paid for the option agreement may be forfeited. The terms of the Lease Option Purchase agreement usually describe how the house will be financed, at what interest rate, and the selling price. The selling price may be set in advance of the actual contract date. This is generally done by using an escalator clause that allows the seller to increase the sales price to the market value of the home at the date of sale or by adding a specified percent to the market value established at the time the LOP agreement was signed. For example, suppose Jones enters into a one year LOP agreement with Campbell to purchase his home. The stipulation is that Jones will pay 3 percent above the current market value of $55,500. This would mean that if the market value at the end of the LOP agreement period declined to $54,500 because of a sagging economy, Jones would have to pay $57,165 for the home if he decided to purchase the home ($55,500 market value at time of LOP agreement plus $1,665, 3 percent of the market value of home). Jones would, in essence, pay $2,665 more than the current market value. Jones also agreed to pay the regular monthly rent of $350 plus $175 per month for the option to purchase the home. If Jones decides not to purchase the home, he would forfeit the $2,100 he paid for the option.

Lease Option Purchase agreements must be planned carefully, and the contract must be properly worded. The buyer should be totally aware of the negative ramifications that could occur from buying a home with a LOP agreement. The method used to determine the sales price at the end of the term should be clearly described. The disposition of the option money should be understood. What happens to the option money should the buyer decide not to buy? Will the seller return a specified percentage of the option money to the buyer? What financial adjustments will be made in the contract for home improvements made by the buyer? These are questions that must be negotiated and incorporated into the LOP agreement. In the preceding case, if there were no conditions placed on the option money as to how it should be applied should the buyer fail to purchase the home, a dispute could occur that could result in costly litigation. To be safe, Jones should include a provision that allows him to purchase the home at the prevailing market value at the time of the sale. This would assure Jones that he would not be overbuying. Also, Jones should negotiate terms that would allow him to add the amount of money spent for home improvements to his down payment. For example, if Jones spent $1,500 for a new roof, this amount should be included in his down payment. In addition, Jones should be aggressive and assertive in negotiating that a specified percentage of the option money be returned should conditions and circumstances that were beyond his control develop to prevent him from buying the home.

LOP agreements can be extremely advantageous to homebuyers, especially those who have compound problems such as lack of funds for the down payment and serious credit deficiencies that require months to correct. For example, a homebuyer who has several collection accounts, slow credit, and a judgment against him could benefit from purchasing a home with a LOP agreement. Assume that Nelson took Dawson to court for failing to pay a debt and obtained a judgement. Dawson also has two outstanding collection accounts that were assigned to collection agencies by his creditors. Dawson is also two months behind with one of his charge accounts. If Dawson entered into an eighteen-month LOP agreement to purchase a home, he would have ample time to develop a financial management plan in which he could take corrective measures to improve his credit rating. The judgment could be corrected by Dawson negotiating a payment plan with the creditor or paying off the judgment and requesting that the creditor send a written letter to the credit reporting agency informing them that the debt has been paid off. Dawson may also request the creditor to ask the credit reporting agency to remove the deficiency from his report. He can correct the slow credit deficiency by paying the accounts several months ahead of their due dates and maintaining this payment schedule for the duration of the LOP agreement. The two collection account deficiencies could be corrected by contacting both creditor and the collection agencies and developing a plan to either reinstate the account with the creditors or to make arrangements with the collection agencies to pay the delinquent accounts. If the creditors agree to reinstatement plans, Dawson should request that a letter be sent to both the credit reporting agency and the collection agency requesting that the deficiency be deleted. It is generally more difficult to get a collection agency to request the reporting agency remove credit deficiencies; therefore, Dawson's contacts should be with the credit managers or someone in a higher position that has the authority to make such a decision. The creditor would be more likely to agree if Dawson paid the total amount of the bill or a substantial part of it with a formalized plan to pay off the balance within a specified time.

The LOP agreement can be an ideal way of buying a home. The seller and buyer can create terms that are very flexible. The buyer should always have someone to act on his behalf so that the proper terms can be negotiated.

30

The Pitfalls of Buying a Home with a Land Sales Contract

The contract of sale is the basic legal instrument that is used in virtually all real estate transactions. The land sales contract, unlike the basic real estate contract, is invariably the riskiest methods of financing a home. It can create a variety of legal problems for the buyer, especially if the seller does not use a title company for managing and servicing the transaction. The land sales contract is a condition where the buyer and a seller agree upon specific terms, such as length of terms, interest rates, monthly installments, and time when the seller must convey deed to the buyer. The land sales contract will have a conditional provision that compels the seller to execute a deed to the buyer after a partial or full performance is completed. This may be when the buyer pays all or a specified percentage of the sales price. If the property is encumbered by an existing mortgage, a description of the mortgage terms and the name of the mortgagee should be stated clearly in the land sales contract. In addition, the contract should specify who will receive the contract payments and how the contract payments will be received. The homebuyer should demand that a title company be used to service the contract while it is in effect. The conditions under which the deed will be conveyed to the buyer should also be expressed clearly to avoid misunderstandings.

The conditional provision protects the buyer against unscrupulous sellers. Under this provision, the seller must convey legal title after a specified amount of the purchase price has been paid. One of the major problems and abuses of the land sales contract transactions occurs when a seller acts as trustee and beneficiary. The seller in this situation would collect the payments and perform all the necessary accounting functions, such as paying the impounds, taxes, and hazard insurance. It is easy for the seller to misapply the monthly payments. There are cases where buyers have paid on property for years with virtually little going toward reducing the principal balance, because the seller comingled the monthly payments with his own personal funds. There are other incidents where the buyers have paid substantially more than the agreed sales price of the property. The land sales contract is usually the only way some buyers will ever get the opportuntiy of buying a home. If they are properly administered by the appropriate agency or institution that specializes in servicing land sales contracts, homebuyers would enjoy a degree of protection they would not have if the seller were servicing his own real estate transaction.

Another situation that complicates the real estate land sales contract is when the seller has a land sales contract plus a first mortgage on the property. In this case, the buyer has to be aware of the three different encumbrances that would be on the property. The first encumbrance would be the first mortgage on the home; the second encumbrance would be the land sales contract the seller used to purchase the home from the original owner; the third encumbrance would be the land sales contract that the homebuyer entered into with the seller to purchase the home.

The following schedule illustrates the complications that could exist when a home has several encumbrances involving land sales contracts.

Schedule of Encumbrances

ENCUMBRANCE	LOAN BALANCE	MONTHLY INSTALLMENTS
Supreme Mortgage Company	$35,500	$250.00
First Land Sales Contract (Seller)	$25,300	$195.00
Second Land Sales Contract (Buyer)	$20,500	$150.00

Three payments would have to be made to three different parties; therefore, it is essential that a title company be used to disperse the funds in accordance with the land sales contracts and mortgage. Using a title company would assure the buyer that payments are being made on a timely basis to the appropriate parties. The land sales contract should state that the seller is selling his *"buyer interest" in the property and that the contract is subjected to an existing land sales contract and mortgage.* The preceding situation could be avoided by the buyer replacing all three encumbrances with a new mortgage. This would eliminate the risks and restrictions that are associated with the land sales contract. This method of financing homes is very common with homebuyers who have limited funds and credit deficiencies and cannot qualify for traditional financing methods. Many of the homes sold on land sales contracts are older homes that have been overpriced. They are purchased by buyers who have difficulties meeting lenders' home loan underwriting standards. Land sales contracts usually carry a much higher interest rate than other real estate financing instruments.

The disadvantage of buying property with a land sales contract is that the buyer is generally prohibited from borrowing money to make home repairs or improvements. Most land sales contracts will impose restraints on the buyers; therefore, it is important for the buyers to have their own attorneys to review or perhaps write provisions into the contract that will give the buyers flexibility. Restrictive clauses that prohibit the buyers from leasing the property without the consent of the seller are common provisions found in many land sales contracts. These types of constraints place limits on what buyers can do with the homes they have purchased. Buyers should be aware of constraints that reduce their options and negotiate for more attractive terms.

Another disadvantage of the land sales contract is that the property can be repossessed quickly, because the deed is usually not conveyed to the buyers until a substantial part or all of the sales price has been paid. The deed is held by an escrow company or title company and not recorded as required when using traditional mortgages and trust deeds. When a payment is missed and not paid within the specified time in accordance with the terms of the land sales contract, the title company may initiate dispossession action against the buyer and evict them from the property. The down payment that was paid, including the installments and appreciated value of the home, would be lost.

31

The Reverse Annuity Mortgage (RAM) (Home Equity Conversion)

Many elderly homeowners living on fixed incomes have extreme financial difficulties maintaining a decent standard of living. The Home Equity Conversion Mortgage is an instrument that will, in effect, change the substantial equity that has been accumulated in their homes into monthly annuities or a one-time cash lump sum combined with monthly annuity payments. The development of Home Equity Conversion Mortgages will provide elderly homeowners with the opportunity of increasing their monthly incomes, thus enabling them to live more comfortably and to become more independent. Home Equity Conversion Mortgages are in the infancy stage and are being modified to cover any unforeseen variables and conditions that may impose hardships on elderly homeowners. Home Equity Conversion Mortgages, like other traditional mortgages, are ideal for homeowners who meet certain conditions and circumstances. They are not designed to meet the needs of all elderly homeowners. Before deciding to use a Home Equity Conversion Mortgage, the homeowner should make a realistic assessment of his specific condition and circumstances. There are several variations of the Home Equity Conversion plan. They should be scrutinized carefully for their total effect. A determination should be made concerning the positive impact that the plan will have on the homeowner's specific problems.

The Reverse Annuity Mortgage (RAM) is actually a loan that is designed to pay the elderly homeowner monthly advances for a specified term of years, such as five, ten, or fifteen. The loan requires that the homeowners retain a certain percent of their equity, such as 20 percent. In essence, the equity retainment of the RAM has the same effect as the loan-to-value ratio in a home equity loan where the homeowner can only borrow up to 70 or 80 percent of the equity accumulated in the home. At the end of the loan period, the loan plus accrued interest must be paid. The RAM also has a due-on-sale provision in which the loan becomes due when the property is sold. Title to the property, however, remains with the homeowner.

If the home increases substantially in value prior to the expiration term of the loan, the homeowner may be in a financial position to repay the loan fully and obtain another one. Assume that an elderly homeowner has a home that has a market value of $55,500 with no outstanding mortgage balance. Although the homeowners received an increase in monthly income by obtaining a RAM loan, which enabled him to increase his living standards, the loan will have to be repaid at the end of the term. The homeowner will then be confronted with a drastic reduction in income, which will invariably force him either to sell his homes or renegotiate another RAM loan that is proportionate with the equity balance in his home. If the homeowner makes arrangements on a timely basis, he may be able to sell his home and obtain the remaining equity in a lump sum. He would then be eligible for subsidized rental housing that would be within his income capacity.

The homeowner could also participate in the other version of the home equity conversion plan, should he decide not to obtain a RAM loan. The Sales Leaseback Plan is different from the RAM plan. Under this plan, the homeowner enters into an agreement with the lender or investor to sell the home, who in turn leases it back to the homeowner. The leaseback plan is extremely complicated and is still being modified to include various provisions such as payment of taxes, insurance, and maintenance. Provisions also include types of financial arrangements for buying the homeowner's equity and methods and conditions of ascertaining rent payments.

The Sales Leaseback Plan includes many variables that determine the amount of the loan payments made to the homeowner. Each transaction is based upon individual conditions and circumstances. Items that affect the amount of the loan payments and terms of the loan include life expectancy of the homeowner, projected repair costs, inflation, increases in insurance and taxes, and appreciation of the market value of the home. All of these factors have to be projected and translated into dollars before the monthly loan payments can be ascertained. Many elderly homeowners are reluctant to use this type of equity conversion plan because it deprives them of the ability to leave a legacy to their children or other relatives. The city of Buffalo, New York, sponsored an innovative Home Equity Conversion plan known as HELP (Home Equity Living Plans) that has been funded by HUD. The HELP program has several Home Equity Conversion plans that guarantee elderly homeowners monthly cash annuity payments. They are also allowed to remain in their homes for the rest of their lives without paying for home maintenance, taxes, and insurance. The homeowners enter into an agreement with HELP that create a life estate in the home that allows them to live in the home until their death. This agreement is referred to as a split equity arrangement, where the lender or investor buys the remainder right of the homeowner. Upon the death of the homeowner, the title passes to HELP.

The Home Equity Conversion Plans, RAM, and the Sales Leaseback Plan should be carefully evaluated. There are advantages and disadvantages to both plans. The homeowner should realistically evaluate his needs and should have a clear understanding of the Equity Conversion Plans. Ideal conditions under which the Home Equity Conversion Plans would be appropriate are depicted by the following illustrations. Assume that an elderly homeowner plans to move into subsidized housing for the elderly in five years. By participating in the Sales Leaseback Plan, the homeowner could receive an initial lump sum cash payment and lifetime monthly annuities that would start at the end of the loan period. This leaseback plan would allow the homeowner to remain in his home without enduring the financial hardship of taking care of the property.

The Leaseback Plan, like the RAM, is not designed to meet the needs of all elderly homeowners, especially if the homeowner's intention is to leave the home to his children. Both plans will allow elderly homeowners to capitalize on the silent and inactive investments that could immensely improve their living standards at a time when their incomes have been reduced significantly. Elderly homeowners who need a temporary increase in their incomes until the occurrence of specific events, but wish to leave the property to their heirs or sell it would benefit from the RAM loan. To illustrate, assume that a homeowner is planning to move into an elderly housing complex in three years, but needs additional income to live comfortably, to give his children money for their education, or to pay off overdue medical bills. This homeowner would benefit from participating in a RAM loan program. He could realize his financial objective of providing funds for their children education, paying off medical bills, or increasing his incomes by participating in the Sales Leaseback Program or the RAM loan program. A complete assessment of conditions and needs must be made prior to participating in a Home Equity Conversion Loan Plan. They can be extremely beneficial, providing the conditions and circumstances are corollated with the homeowner's needs.

32

Owner Carryback (OCB) Arrangements

The classified section of the newspaper is full of advertisements with the letters "OWC" (Owner Will Carry). The Owner Carryback arrangements are invariably the most versatile purchase programs of all mortgage instruments. The scope and range of the various Owner Carryback Arrangements are limited only by the imagination and innovative minds of the buyer and sellers. There have been real estate transactions where the buyer exchanged personal property as part of the down payment in a carryback arrangement. Down payments have included antiques, automobiles, boats, stocks, bonds, and even treasury bills.

A typical illustration of an Owner Carryback Arrangement is where a buyer includes a boat, valued at $7,500, and $3,000 cash as part of the down payment on a $75,500 home that has an existing 8½ percent, $35,500 mortgage with monthly mortgage payments of $367. The buyer includes the $7,500 boat and $3,000 cash as the down payment and agrees to give the seller a $29,500 second mortgage at 10 percent interest amortized over thirty years; but due in 5 years with monthly payments of $258.00. The buyer's house payment would be the first mortgage payment, $367.00, and the second mortgage payment would be $258.00, to make a total payment of $625.00. If the buyer elects to obtain new financing with a 10 percent down payment ($7,500), using the current interest rate of 13 percent, the buyer would finance $68,000 ($75,500 sales price − $7,500 down payment). The mortgage payments would be $752. The difference between the Owner Carryback Arrangement of $625, and new financing at the current interest rate of $725 is $127.00. The buyer would save $127 per month by using the OCB financing arrangement.

There, however, are disadvantages as well as advantages to the OCB. The buyer can reduce the mortgage payment on the mortgage.

The expense of paying the exorbitant closing costs can be eliminated; since the buyer is assuming the existing mortgage, homebuyers with limited income would be able to purchase a home. Many down payment variations can be negotiated between the buyer and seller.

There are also some disadvantages to the OCB arrangement. Since there is a second mortgage on the home, it may be difficult to borrow money to make improvements or make repairs. Also, if the buyer used a balloon mortgage, as in the illustration, it may be difficult to refinance the balloon payment when due in five years. In addition, if the lender enforces the due-on-sales clause in the first mortgage, the home may be beyond the financial capacity of the buyer.

The above illustration represents only one of many OCB arrangements. The buyers are encouraged to consult an attorney or counseling agency for interpretation of the various forms of OCB arrangements.

The Owner's Carryback offers an opportunity to homebuyers who have the down payment but lack the credit capacity to obtain a new mortgage. OCBs, however, can be extremely risky for homebuyers who lack understanding of the various implications. A homebuyer would be very wise to consult a real estate attorney or another objective real estate broker to interpret the contractual obligations.

To delineate the complexity of OCBs, consider the following example. A homeowner sells his home for $85,500. There is a $45,500 8 percent outstanding mortgage. The homebuyer has only $10,000 down payment. The homeowner accepts the $10,000, takes out a $20,000 second mortgage, and creates a $10,500 five-year interest only balloon. The homeowner has three mortgage payments to make—first mortgage, second mortgage, and the balloon mortgage. The risk is that the homebuyer may not be able to refinance the balloon when due, hence the seller can foreclose.

An Owner Carryback is the only way some buyers can purchase a home. Properly written and arranged, carrybacks can be beneficial to both the buyer and the seller. The complications occur when the arrangements and configurations of the contract and mortgages fall outside of the buyer's financial capacity. Homebuyers should consult a real estate attorney or other real estate professional to develop the language used in the contract and to interpret the effects of the contractual terms. Many homeowners have lost their homes because they did not understand the implications of the real estate language used in the contract.

To illustrate what happens to homebuyers who allow themselves to become involved in an Owner Carryback without the advice of real estate professionals, assume that Edwards purchased a $85,500 home, with an existing $20,500 mortgage, with a mortgage payment of $375 per month. Edwards has a gross monthly income of $1,500. He agrees to pay $9,500 down. The seller needs all the money he can get from the sale, because he is buying another larger home and plans on going

125

into the restaurant business. The seller has $65,000 equity in the home ($85,500 selling price less $20,500 existing mortgage). He takes out a $45,500 second mortgage with 14½ percent interest for fifteen years. The monthly payment on the second mortgage is $621. Edwards agrees to assume the first and second mortgages. The seller agrees to give Edwards an Owner's Carryback contract with the following terms: $10,000 interest only for one year at 10 percent interest. This configuration of mortgages and contract will impose a serious financial burden on Edwards. His total mortgage payments will be $1,079 ($375 on the first mortgage + $621, the second mortgage, and $83 on the interest only balloon contract). The mortgage payment represents 71 percent of Edwards' gross income. His debt-income ratio exceeds the norm. If this condition should become aggravated due to the occurrence of unanticipated incidents, Edwards could easily default on the mortgages and contract. He would, therefore, lose the $9,500 that was paid down on the home unless the home is sold. One significant factor that Edwards must be aware of is that the $10,000 balloon contract will become due in one year. This means that Edwards will have to refinance the $10,000 balloon contract. The fact that his debt-income ratio is already in a precarious financial state means most lenders will probably reject his application for a loan. This will leave Edwards with the option of increasing his income or liquidating some of his assets to reduce the debt-income ratio. With a lower debt-income ratio, he may be able to qualify for a loan to pay off the balloon contract. The other option is to sell the home to recapture his equity. Owner's Carrybacks should be used only by buyers with specific debt-income structures. It definitely should not be used to obtain a larger, exclusive home whose costs exeed the buyers' financial limitations.

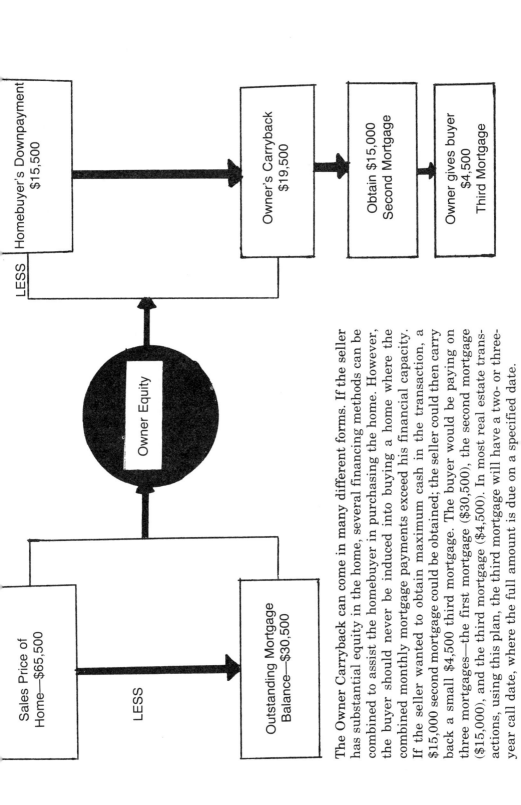

Sales Price of Home—$65,500		Homebuyer's Downpayment $15,500
LESS		LESS

Owner Equity

| Outstanding Mortgage Balance—$30,500 | | Owner's Carryback $19,500 |

Obtain $15,000 Second Mortgage

Owner gives buyer $4,500 Third Mortgage

The Owner Carryback can come in many different forms. If the seller has substantial equity in the home, several financing methods can be combined to assist the homebuyer in purchasing the home. However, the buyer should never be induced into buying a home where the combined monthly mortgage payments exceed his financial capacity. If the seller wanted to obtain maximum cash in the transaction, a $15,000 second mortgage could be obtained; the seller could then carry back a small $4,500 third mortgage. The buyer would be paying on three mortgages—the first mortgage ($30,500), the second mortgage ($15,000), and the third mortgage ($4,500). In most real estate transactions, using this plan, the third mortgage will have a two- or three-year call date, where the full amount is due on a specified date.

33

Benefits of the
Renegotiable Mortgage (REM)

Lenders, like all businesses, try to diversify their services to home-buyers in order to expand their business and increase their interest revenue. The Renegotiable Mortgage (REM) is a mortgage instrument that offers flexibility to homebuyers. Although new in name, the concept of the REM goes back to post–Civil War years when wealthy landowners sold land to ex-slaves for a percentage of their crops. This practice was called sharecropping. The landowner would receive a specified percentage of the revenue received by the sharecropper from selling his crops. The landowner had a provision in the contract that would allow for adjustment for an increase or decrease in the crops' yield. The REM is renegotiated at specified intervals, such as every three or five years. The REM offers several advantages to the homebuyer. If the interest should decrease significantly prior to the time of the renegotiation, the homebuyer's mortgage payment would decrease. For example, if the interest rate at the time of the initial financing on a $62,500 mortgage is 16½ percent, the mortgage payment would be $865. If the interest decreases to 13 percent, the mortgage payment would be reduced to $692 per month, for a savings of $173.

Another benefit of the REM is that, generally, the homebuyer may not have to pay expensive points for refinancing the loan. Unlike other mortgage instruments that will refinance, at the most, 90 percent of the market value of the home, the REM will normally finance 100 percent of the mortgage balance. To illustrate, if the homebuyer has a home with a mortgage balance of $65,500 and a market value of $70,000, to refinance with a 90 percent loan to value, the homebuyer would only be able to refinance .90 × $70,000 = $63,000. Since the homebuyer has a mortgage of $65,500, an initial deposit of $2,500 would have to be made before the homeowner could refinance to take advantage of a lower interest rate.

The major differences between the Adjusted Rate Mortgage (ARM) and the Renegotiable Mortgage (REM) is that the ARM interest is adjusted to a floating index, while the REM is adjusted to the current and prevailing interest rate at the time of refinancing. Because the ARM interest rate is adjusted to a floating index during the year, negative amortization can occur where the entire mortgage payment is applied to pay the interest. The principal balance may even increase. The Renegotiable Mortgage normally will never have negative amortization, because the interest rate remains constant until the loan is renegotiated.

The Renegotiable Mortgage (REM) may actually cause the homebuyers' monthly mortgage payments to increase. To illustrate, assume that a homebuyer buys a home with a 13 percent, thirty-year, $72,000 mortgage. If the homebuyer's REM is renegotiated every three years and the interest rate increases from 13 to 16 percent in three years, the monthly payments could increase substantially. The mortgage payment at 13 percent interest for thirty years on a $72,000 mortgage is $796. The payment on the new 16 percent mortgage would be approximately $965, allowing for adjustments for a slight reduction in the mortgage balance. There would be an increase of $169 in the mortgage payment.

The homebuyer should check the costs of renegotiating a new mortgage. Expenditures that should be checked by the homebuyer are: (a) Will the homeowner have to pay points for refinancing? (b) Will an appraisal be required? (c) What other loan fees will the homeowner have to pay for refinancing? These are important questions with which the homebuyer should be concerned. If the interest rate increases, the homebuyer may be faced with mortgage payments that exceed his financial capacity. It is therefore important for the homebuyer to maintain a low debt-income ratio so that money will be available to compensate for the increase in mortgage payments.

The Renegotiable Mortgage is similar to the Roll Over Mortgage (ROM) used in other countries, especially Canada. It is one that can be highly beneficial to the homebuyer. The Roll Over Mortgage is rewritten at specified intervals. For example, a ROM that expires at the end of ten years is rewritten at the prevailing interest rate. The REM interest rates generally change on a more frequent basis. REMs may be rewritten every two, three, or five years, contingent upon the terms negotiated with the lenders. The Renegotiable Mortgages can be a disadvantage as well as an advantage to homebuyers. It is, therefore, important for the homebuyer to compare other financing methods with the REM.

The following schedule compares the REM with other mortgages. Assume that the interest increased by three percent in three years.

129

The mortgage payment is based on a $70,000, thirty-year mortgage at 14 percent interest. The prevailing interest rate in three years is assumed to be 16 percent, and the mortgage is renegotiated every three years.

Mortgage Payment Comparison Schedule

Year	REM 2% Decrease	REM 2% Increase	Standard Fixed Rate Mortgage 14%	Interest Buy-Down 3-2-1
1	$829	$829	$829	$667
2	$829	$829	$829	$718
3	$829	$829	$829	$772
4	$720	$941	$829	$825

The schedule shows the effect of an increase or decrease in the REM interest rates. Should the inflation cause the interest to increase, the REM will increase. A deflation will have the opposite effect: the mortgage payment will decrease. In the fourth year, the REM payments will decrease, as indicated in column 1, or increase, as shown in column 2, while the Standard Fixed Rate Mortgage remains constant throughout the life of the mortgage. Under the 3-2-1 interest buy-down plan, the mortgage payments would increase each year until the fourth year. The payments would then remain constant during the remaining life of the mortgage. Like other variable rate mortgages, the REM should be used only by those homebuyers who have financial income structures and managerial skills to make the appropriate fiscal adjustments to the increase in payments should the interest rate increase.

34

The Reserve Account Mortgage

Real estate financing has become extremely diversified. Thirty years ago, buying a home was simple. However, with the advent of high interest rates and the perpetual escalation in the cost of construction, new real estate financing methods were designed and utilized by developers, homeowners, and homebuyers. In fact, financing a home is almost like buying a car. There are so many financing models, it is difficult to make a selection as to what financing method is compatible with the homebuyers' financial capacity. The Federal National Mortgage Association (Fannie Mae) has endorsed and is utilizing an innovative real estate instrument that, in effect, will enable many homebuyers who lack the initial down payment to purchase a home. This real estate instrument is known as the Reserve Account Mortgage. The concept of this financing plan has been around for a long time and has been used surreptitiously by real estate agents and homebuyers in financing homes. Many state real estate regulations have prohibited or discouraged this method of financing homes in the past. Under this real estate financing design, a homebuyer will be able to purchase a home with a maximum loan of $103,300. The unique feature of the Reserve Account Mortgage is that it allows the builder, a relative, a friend, or a real estate broker to deposit 5 percent in an interest-bearing, fully refundable savings account. The special account will be operated and controlled by the lender making the loan to the homebuyer. The homebuyers are not required to make the usual down payment, hence are enabled to move into a home by paying only a portion of the required closing and escrow costs. The interest-bearing savings account created provides a temporary equity that acts as a form of insurance protection for Fannie Mae should the homebuyer default on the mortgage. In case of a default by the buyer, Fannie Mae will file claim to the money deposited in the savings account by the contributor. In addition, a 2½ percent loss reserve fee is required. This is a one-time charge that is based on the loan amount. It represents another form of insurance for Fannie Mae. The interest rate charged is lower than market rate interest. The rate is tied in with Fannie Mae's three- and five-year Adjustable Rate Mortgages. The builder can reduce the interest further by buying the interest down from the adjusted rate. Assume that the current market rate is 14 percent and the Fannie Mae's adjusted rate is 12½ percent. By using a 3-2-1 buy-down plan, the builder could sell homes with an interest rate of 9½ percent the first year.

One of the most interesting and innovative things about the Reserve Account Mortgage is that it allows a third party or contributor to put up money without the buyer having to repay it back at a later date. There are many documented cases where homebuyers have been forced into precarious financial predicaments that resulted in their losing their homes because they could not repay loans that they made to pay the required down payment. The Reserve Account Mortgage will eliminate this financial burden. The contributor to the interest-bearing savings account could get all of the money deposited, plus interest, in three years. The Federal National Mortgage Association requires that money be retained in the savings account for at least three years until the loan balance decreases to 90 percent of the appraised value of the home. For example, if a person buys a home for $74,500 and in three years, it appraised for $83,500, the lender would refund the money deposited, plus interest, to the contributor. Ninety percent of $83,500 (the appraised value of the home) is $75,150. The home increased by $9,000 in three years, thus reducing the loan balance to less than 90 percent of the appraisal value. When this condition occurs, the contributor would be entitled to the 5 percent money that was contributed toward the interest-bearing savings account. The homebuyer should be extremely cautious before using a Reserve Account Mortgage to finance a home, especially if the builder uses an interest reduction or 3-2-1 buy-down plan. The mortgage payments could increase as much as 30 percent in four years. This drastic increase in monthly mortgage payments could cause the homebuyer dire financial problems. As an illustration, assume that the homebuyer purchased a home with an Adjusted Rate Mortgage at 12½ percent interest. The amount of the mortgage was $75,000. If the builder used a 3-2-1 buy-down plan, the interest rate for the first year would be 9½ percent (12½ percent adjusted rate interest minus 3 percent builders' buy-down plan). The mortgage payment, consisting of only the principal and interest on a $75,000 mortgage, is $631. Beginning the fourth year of the 3-2-1 buy-down plan, the interest would increase to 12½ percent. If the index used to determine the adjusted interest rate also increased by 1 percent, the effective overall increase would be 4 percent, going from 9½ to 13½ percent. The monthly mortgage payment at

13½ percent on the remaining loan balance of approximately $74,000 would be $857, compared to only $631 at 9½ percent. This constitutes a substantial 36 percent increase in monthly mortgage payments. The homebuyer should assure himself that his income will increase proportionately with the monthly mortgage payments.

Another negative aspect of the Reserve Mortgage Account is that some contributors, builders, real estate brokers, and sellers may be encouraged to increase the price of the home to maximize their profits and cover their initial cash investments to the interest-bearing savings account required by Fannie Mae. This clandestine strategy could be perpetrated easily by the seller or builder. Assume that the seller has a home that he planned to sell for $60,500. The seller decides to use a Reserve Account Mortgage to finance the home, because the buyer did not have money to pay the down payment. The seller increased the price of the home by $3,025, (.05 × $60,500) to cover the 5 percent cash deposit required by the Federal National Mortgage Association. There is no way a buyer can prevent a seller from including the required deposit in the sales price of the home. The most effective way of controlling the seller's actions is for the buyer to check the prices of other similar homes in the neighborhood and negotiate effectively.

35

The Shared Appreciation Mortgage (SAM)

As the interest rate goes up along with the purchase price of a home, the affordability of the home goes down. The American dream of owning a home is fast become an impossibility. The dropout rate of homebuyers from the housing market is increasing faster than ever. Inflation has contributed immensely to this housing dilemma. Salaries have not kept up proportionately with the interest rate and the cost of construction. When these conditions prevail, various innovative financial plans to assist homebuyers to qualify began to appear. The Shared Appreciation Mortgage, better known as SAM, is one such real estate financial instrument that is being utilized presently throughout the nation. In fact, companies have developed whose sole operation is to assist homebuyers who are unable to use traditional financial plans to purchase a home. Homebuyers must realize that investment companies specializing in SAMs are in business to generate income and profits for their investors. SAMs will be written carefully to contain many provisions that may appear nebulous or unclear to homebuyers. Although the SAM is a relatively new approach in financing homes, it has been used widely in commercial real estate transactions, especially the financing of apartment complexes.

The SAM concept is really a simple approach to financing a home. The difficulties arise when investors incorporate various provisions that could impose financial hardships on unsuspecting buyers. The SAM concept can be explained by using the equity sharing principle. The SAM investor, in essence, becomes a partner with the homebuyer. They purchase the home together as co-mortgagors, with both sharing a percentage of the mortgage payments, taxes, insurance, and major repairs. Title to the property is taken out as tenants-in-common without rights of survivorship. This means that upon the death of one co-mortgagor, title passes to the co-mortgagor's designated heirs instead of going to the surviving co-mortgagor. The homebuyer should always get a professional such as a real estate attorney or another real estate professional to interpret the SAM's provisions.

There are certain SAM provisions of which the homebuyer should have a crystal clear understanding. All SAMs will have a maturity clause that causes the loan to become due at some specified future date. These maturity dates vary according to the policies of the company investing in the home. A typical maturity date would be five to seven years. The homeowner would have to buy the investor's share in seven years. This may not be financially feasible for the homebuyer, unless his financial capacity has made a substantial increase during the period of the loan. Another provision that the homebuyer must be aware of is the provision that explains how costs for regular maintenance and needed major repairs are to be shared and arranged. The SAM should be spelled out in detail. The procedures and time required to make the necessary repairs must be established clearly. For example, suppose an accident occurred in which the water heater needed to be replaced. The homeowner should be aware of the flexibility of the repair provision. Could the homeowner be able to call a contractor to have the heater replaced and submit a bill and be reimbursed? How much time is required for the investor to compensate the homebuyer for his expense incurred in making the repairs? What kind of notification is necessary, and when must it be submitted to the investor? These are examples of questions that the provisions must delineate clearly.

Another provision that can cause many problems that may result in the homebuyer being forced to sell his equity to the investor is the delinquency provison. This provision should explain the effects and repercussions that will occur if the homebuyer becomes delinquent with his share of the mortgage payment. Information such as the amount of late charge and the date on which late fees may be accessed should be specified. The homeowner should also be aware of any clauses and provisions under which the investor can buy his equity, such as a provision that allows the investor to buy the homeowner's equity if he becomes three months delinquent with his share of the payment or allows the investor to obtain title if the homeowner caused the property to be affected by economic waste as a result of a lack of maintenance of the property.

To illustrate how the SAM operates, assume that a homebuyer enters into an agreement with a SAM investor in which a $75,500 home is purchased with a thirty-year fixed-rate mortgage. The interest rate is 14½ percent for thirty years. Other monthly expenses include, property taxes, forty dollars; insurance, twenty dollars; and investor's service fee, thirty percent of total mortgage payments, $268 ($892 × .30). The homebuyer agrees to a 50 percent shared equity plan. The investor will pay 50 percent of all expenses, but will get 50 percent of the appreciated value of the home when the home is sold before or at the end of the loan term. The following schedule shows each co-mortgagor's share of the expense of the home using the preceding information.

Co-Mortgagor's Share of Housing Expense

	Expense	Buyer	Co-Mortgagor
Down Payment	$7,550	$3,775	$3,775
Mortgage Payment	$ 832	$416	$ 416
Property Taxes	$40	$20	20
Insurance	$20	$10	10
Investor Service Fee		$ 268	0
Closing Cost Estimate (2% of Sales Price)	$1,510	$755	$ 755

The homebuyer's share of the mortgage would be $714. This amount includes the investor's service fee. The investor's share would be $446, which includes the following: 50 percent of the mortgage payment, $416; half of the taxes, $20; and $10 for insurance. If the homebuyer had to pay the entire mortgage payment, he would pay $178 more per month ($892 total mortgage payment less $714, homebuyer's share of the mortgage payment). If the lender uses a 30 percent housing expense ratio, the homebuyer would need a gross monthly income of $2,973, ($892 total mortgage payment divided by .30, required lender's housing expense ratio). By using a SAM to finance the home, the homebuyer would need only $2,380 monthly income, which is approximately $593 per month less income. In effect, it takes less income to qualify for the home using the SAM as a financing instrument.

The disadvantage of the SAM is that if the homebuyer has a five-year call provision in the mortgage, he would have to purchase the investor's equity. To illustrate the financial difficulties the homebuyer may encounter, assume that the home appreciated in value by $10,000. It would then have a market value of $85,500. If the homebuyer purchased the investor's equity at the end of the term, he would have to borrow approximately $9,250 (current market value, $85,500, less $67,000, estimated current loan balance). Assume that the homebuyer took out a second mortgage for fifteen years with an interest rate of 16 percent. The monthly payment on the second mortgage would be $137. The total monthly expense that the homebuyer would have would be $1,029. This amount includes the total mortgage payment of $892, plus the $137 for the second mortgage. The amount of the monthly income the homebuyer would need to maintain the mortgage would be $3,430. Unless the homebuyer's income increased substantially during the five-year loan period, he may encounter difficulties trying to borrow enough money to buy the investor's equity. If such a condition should occur, the homebuyer would have to sell his equity to the investor or the house would have to be sold. The positive side or the advantage of using the SAM to finance the home is that the homebuyer would have created $9,250 savings by buying the home. He would have also enjoyed the tax benefits of deducting the property taxes and interest from his income, thereby reducing his taxable income. Another disadvantage is that the homebuyer has to get approval from the investor in order to make major home improvements. He usually cannot take out a second mortgage for any desired purpose. In other words, there are restraints incorporated in a SAM mortgage that inhibit the homebuyer and lock him into a financing plan where his equity is frozen until the home is sold or the loan expires.

HUD SHARED EQUITY POLICIES

The shared equity approach to buying a home has been examined very closely by HUD to protect the occupant mortgagor's interest. HUD has established the following policies with which the investor co-mortgagor must be in compliance:

A. The sharing of equity upon the disposition of the property shall be the same percentage as the percentage of the monthly mortgage payment made by each co-mortgagor.
B. The co-mortgagor in possession of the property has the right to buy the investor co-mortgagor's equity at any time upon thirty days' written notice.
C. The investor co-mortgagor may force sale or refinance the property should the occupant co-mortgagor default on the loan. The investor would then acquire the right to obtain the occupant co-mortgagor's interest in the property.
D. The sales price of the property shall be determined by an appraisal made by a HUD-approved appraiser. The party may circumvent the HUD appraisal by arriving at a mutual sales price.
E. Either the occupant co-mortgagor or the investor co-mortgagor may sell his interest in the property after giving the other co-mortgagor a thirty-day written option to purchase the property.
F. In case of shortage in one co-mortgagor's share of the mortgage

payment, the other co-mortgagor may submit the amount of the shortage and recover the shortage upon sale or refinancing of the property, providing the shortage has not been paid.

G. Both co-mortgagors shall share all insurance, maintenance, and major repairs that are based on the equity percentage arrangement.

H. The occupant co-mortgagor has the right to make significant home improvements or alterations only after notifying the investor co-mortgagor. The co-mortgagor may elect to share in the cost of such repairs or allow the appropriate equity adjustments to compensate for the cost upon sale or refinancing the property.

DETERMINING CO-MORTGAGOR SHARE UPON SALE OF PROPERTY OR EXPIRATION OF THE SHARED EQUITY AGREEMENT

Co-mortgagor Share of Down Payment	$3,750
Co-Mortgagor Share of Appreciated Value of Home Assume that the home appreciated in value by $15,000. The co-mortgagor share, ½($10,000), is $5,000.	$5,000
Total Due Co-mortgagor upon Sale of the Home or Expiration of the Shared Equity Agreement	$8,750

UNDERSTANDING THE SHARED EQUITY CONCEPT
OF PURCHASING A HOME

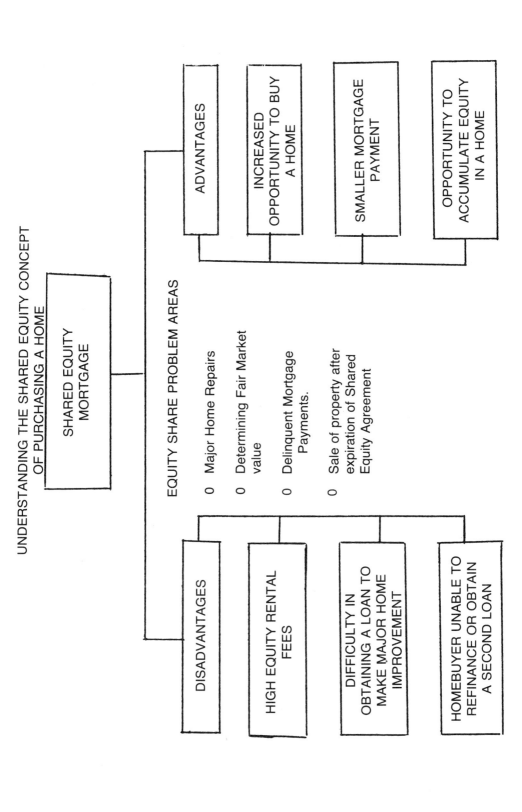

SHARED EQUITY
MORTGAGE

ADVANTAGES

INCREASED
OPPORTUNITY TO BUY
A HOME

SMALLER MORTGAGE
PAYMENT

OPPORTUNITY TO
ACCUMULATE EQUITY
IN A HOME

EQUITY SHARE PROBLEM AREAS

o   Major Home Repairs

o   Determining Fair Market
    value

o   Delinquent Mortgage
    Payments.

o   Sale of property after
    expiration of Shared
    Equity Agreement

DISADVANTAGES

HIGH EQUITY RENTAL
FEES

DIFFICULTY IN
OBTAINING A LOAN TO
MAKE MAJOR HOME
IMPROVEMENT

HOMEBUYER UNABLE TO
REFINANCE OR OBTAIN
A SECOND LOAN

36

The Effects of Using
a Second Mortgage
to Finance a Home

The use of second mortgages in financing homes is becoming extremely popular. In fact, more homebuyers are finding that obtaining a second mortgage is practically the only way that they can afford to buy. This financing technique can be used in many combinations. It is the combination of contracts with mortgages that creates financial problems for both the buyers and sellers. Many innovative financing plans have been created by real estate agents to assist homebuyers to purchase homes. Some of these creative plans should be avoided because they create unreasonably burdensome financial problems for the buyers. Some elderly homeowners are convinced to sell their home on a second mortgage to create a continuous cash flow during their retirement years. The problem arises when a buyer who doesn't have the financial capacity to use a second mortgage is talked into purchasing the home. The homebuyer who lacks the money to purchase the seller's equity may be able to qualify for a second mortgage. The total combined mortgage payments on the first and second mortgages, including the other housing expenses, such as utilities, property taxes, maintenance, and hazardous insurance, should not exceed the lenders' housing expense ratios. These ratios depend upon the borrowers' individual condition and circumstance. For homebuyers with a record of employment instability and credit deficiencies, the lender probably will not make the loan or the loan will be approved with a low debt-income ratio. Homebuyers who have very good credit ratings and a history of stable employment would be more likely to qualify for a second mortgage, even though they may have a high debt-income ratio. Buyers should be aware of real estate sales agents who use a combination of mortgages that cause the combined mortgage payments to increase beyond the homebuyers' financial capacity. As long as the homebuyer stays within his income limits, a second mortgage could be a very good way to finance a home. Second mortgages are very often used by the wrong homebuyers. In many cases, homebuyers with serious credit deficiences buy homes that are beyond their financial limitations.

By combining the first mortgage with a second mortgage, the buyer can generally lower his mortgage payments. Obtaining second mortgages to buy homes is becoming very popular. The buyer may be able to assume an existing mortgage with a lower interest rate. However, the buyer should check with the lender to see if the mortgage is assumable. Assume a homeowner sells a home for $65,500 with an 8 percent assumable mortgage. The existing mortgage is $40,500, with monthly mortgage payments of $316. If the lender requires 10 percent down, $6,550, the buyer would have to get a second mortgage for $18,450 ($65,500 − $47,050). If the current interest rate on a fifteen-year second mortgage is 16 percent, the buyer would then have a total mortgage payment of $585 ($316 first mortgage plus $269 on the second mortgage). Should the homebuyer get a new thirty-year mortgage at a 13 percent interest rate, the payment would be $652 after paying 10 percent down, $6,550, and financing $58,950. The buyer would save sixty-seven dollars by using a combination of a first and second mortgage. As with other mortgage instruments, there are advantages and disadvantages to both the buyer and the seller. The buyer can avoid paying a large sum of money for the seller's equity. In addition, the buyer can eliminate the closing costs, since there are no closing costs involved when a buyer assumes an existing mortgage. The seller is able to sell the house by obtaining his equity with funds provided by a second mortgage. Unless the seller obtains a release from the lender, he is still liable on the first mortgage. There can be many forms and variations of the second mortgage. The buyer should be aware of these variations and the applications.

Lenders are now combining features of the balloon mortgages with second mortgages to make it attractive for homeowners to borrow money. This will also make it possible for the homebuyer to purchase a home with lower combined mortgage payments. Assume that a homeowner sells a home for $55,500 with an existing $25,500 mortgage. The buyer has only $5,000 for a down payment and takes out a 13 percent second mortgage for $25,000 ($30,000 sellers equity less the $5,000 down payment). The $25,000 is amortized over thirty years but due in fifteen years. In effect, the second mortgage is similar to a balloon mortgage and also has a feature of the thirty-year fixed mortgage. The monthly payment on the second mortgage is $277 if the first mortgage has a mortgage payment of $275 per month. The combined first and second mortgage payments would be $552.

The key elements of a good second mortgage are low interest rates and long payment terms. The longer the terms and the lower the interest rate, the smaller the loan payment will be. It is, therefore, possible for the homebuyer to assume a first mortgage with a low interest rate and take out a second mortgage so the total combined mortgage payments would be lower than they would be on a new loan with a higher interest rate. One significant advantage of the second mortgage is that, generally, it will be paid off in fifteen years or less. The homebuyer would then have only the payment on the first mortgage to make.

The average price of a home is rising proportionately faster than homebuyers' incomes. This disparity between the average price of a home and buyers' income has caused a "homebuyer's dropout shock," which has had a detrimental effect on the real estate and the home construction industries. High interest rates combined with the increase in market values of homes has caused second mortgages to become a widely used home financing method. In fact, lenders are now specializing in making second loans on homes. The homebuyers must be creditworthy and meet the lenders' loan standards. These lenders will require that the homebuyers pay a specified percentage of the seller's equity. The purpose of this down payment is to protect the lender and minimize their risks of the buyer's defaulting on either or both the first and second mortgages. With the prices of homes increasing faster then the homebuyer's incomes, the opportunity of buying a home with new financing is fast disappearing. This is the reason why the Adjusted Rate Mortgages and interest reduction plans are so popular. Homebuyers were forced out of the housing market, because the impact of the high interest rates and the high selling price of homes made it financially impossible for them to qualify for new mortgage loans. Because of this, real estate sales agents are encouraging the use of second mortgages, either as an Owner's Carryback or to buy the owner's equity.

37

The Effects of Financing a Home with a Wraparound Mortgage

The competition between lenders for the prospective homebuyer's dollars has caused lenders (including the Federal National Mortgage Association, known as Fannie Mae) to modify and create innovative financing techniques to make mortgage instruments attractive to these buyers. Fannie Mae and other institutional lenders have large portfolios of low-interest home loans. In an effort to reduce these low-interest loans, they have developed and implemented the wraparound mortgage. Since the inception of the wraparound, many prospective homebuyers have been able to purchase homes with lower mortgage payments. Those unable to qualify previously because of high interest rates were able to purchase homes by using the wraparound mortgage to reduce the interest to levels that they could afford.

The wraparound mortgage utilizes the mathematical effect of computing large numbers with smaller numbers that are in the appropriate proportion to produce a decreasing effect on the mortgage interest and mortgage payment. The interest rate is dependent upon two significant factors: the amount of the first mortgage and the sales price of the home or the amount financed. For example, the effect of wrapping a $32,000, 8½ percent mortgage with a $40,000, 14½ percent mortgage is reduction of the overall mortgage rate below 14½ percent. The difference between Fannie Mae wraps and lenders' wraps is that in Fannie Mae wraps, the old lower-interest mortgage is completely eliminated and replaced with a new mortgage with a below market interest rate. The lenders' wraparound mortgage leaves the existing mortgage with the lower interest rate intact. However, the mathematical effects of both mortgages are the same. The advantage of the lenders' wraparound mortgage is that this wrap mortgage is normally paid off in fifteen years, leaving the lower interest loan with a low mortgage payment to pay. Fannie Mae wraps are new thirty-year mortgages that have an extended term. The disadvantage of the lenders' wrap is that a second mortgage will affect the buyer's borrowing ability. If, for instance, the homebuyer wanted to add a swimming pool or a room, he might find it difficult to obtain a loan because of the wraparound mortgage that was used to finance the home. The Federal National Mortgage Association is losing millions of dollars because lenders are processing smaller short-term wrap mortgages and leaving the low-interest Fannie Mae mortgages intact. Under the wrap mortgage, the homebuyer sends one mortgage payment to the lender to cover the first mortgage and the second wrap mortgage. The lender collects the payment and pays on the first mortgage. Fannie Mae is encouraging home-buyers to use their wrap mortgages by enforcing the due-on-sale provision contained in Fannie Mae mortgages.

The sellers and buyers may also create their own wrap mortgages. When this situation occurs, the buyers lack the funds to buy the sellers' equity. A sellers' wraparound mortgage can be created by contracting a title company to service the wrap mortgage. To illustrate how the sellers' wrap works, assume that Baker buys a home from Edwards that costs $73,500. The home has an existing $35,500 mortgage with Supreme Mortgage Company. The existing interest rate is 8 percent, with mortgage payments of $360 per month. Baker pays $8,500 for a down payment, plus the usual closing costs. The amount of the second wrap mortgage is $29,500 ($73,500 sales price of the home less $35,500 existing, plus $8,500 down payment). Baker and Edwards agree to blend the 8 percent old interest rate on the existing mortgage with the current market rate. Assume that the current interest rate is 15½ percent. The new rate of interest on the second wrap mortgage can be calculated by using the following formula, .08(EM) + 15½(WM) ÷ $35,500 + $29,500. Substituting the figures in the formula, the new interest can be determined. .08 × $35,500 + .155 × $29,500 $7,413 ÷ $65,000 = 11 percent The new interest rate is computed as 11 percent. This amount is substantially smaller than the 15½ percent that would be charged at market interest rate, but slightly higher than the 8 percent interest on the existing mortgage. Baker should inquire about the possibility of the loan being called due by Supreme Mortgage Company. If Supreme Mortgage should call the loan due, this would negate the effect of the wraparound mortgage.

Economic conditions have caused FNMA to suffer, because the cost of obtaining money has increased. The higher cost of obtaining money is aggravated by the thousands of low-interest loans that still remain in their portfolio. In essence, the reason for the emergence of FNMA wraparound mortgages is to compensate for the low-interest loans that are still on FNMA's books and to increase the interest yield from new wraparound mortgages.

Wraparound mortgages are increasing in popularity, especially the owners' wrap. This financing method is especially attractive to homebuyers who lack the financial capacity to completely buy the sellers' equity. It is a financing method that must be thoroughly evaluated. The largest impediment to the wraparound mortgage is the due-on-sale provision. The continued existence of the wrap mortgages will depend on how the Supreme Court rules on suits that have been initiated against lenders. In some states, regulations place a limit on how much a lender can increase the interest upon sale of the property. Most real estate agents, including buyers and sellers, would agree that the lenders should be able to increase the interest on low-yielding loans. They, however, believe that a limit on the amount of the increase should be regulated to prevent lenders from unconscionably increasing the interest to a rate that would prevent many prospective buyers from owing a home.

The following mortgage comparison schedule shows that the wraparound mortgage can be an effective mortgage instrument to provide many Americans with the opportunity of acquiring affordable homes:

Mortgage Payment Comparison Schedule

$65,400 Mortgage Amount at 14½ Percent
Interest for 30 Years

	Mortgage Payment
Wraparound Mortgage	
(Interest Computed at 11%)	$622.83
Standard Fixed Rate Mortgage	$800.87
HUD Graduated Payment Mortgage (Plan V)	$668.76
Developers Buy-Down Plan (3% below Market Rate)	$647.66
Adjusted Rate Mortgage (ARM)	$697.99
(2% below Market Rate)	

The statistical information disclosed in the schedule shows that the wraparound mortgages are extremely competitive. They are less costly than many of the popular real estate financing methods used today. The wraps, like other financing methods, should be reviewed prior to use. A real estate attorney or other real estate professional should be consulted to interpret the various effects of the wraparound mortgage. A number of lenders and mortgage companies do a high volume of wraparound mortgages. They have developed guidelines on what kinds of mortgages they will wrap. For example, some mortgage companies require that the buyer pays a certain percentage down. The rationale for this guideline is that homebuyers who pay a substantial amount down have a financial interest to protect. The chance of their defaulting on the loan is less than with those buyers who submit only a small percentage down. Another typical lender policy is that the amount of the loan cannot be more than twice the amount owed on the existing first mortgage. If a seller has an existing mortgage on a home in the amount of $25,500, the lender would finance $51,000 on a wraparound mortgage. The wraparound mortgage can provide an economical way of buying a home. It can also cause the homebuyer serious financial problems. It is, therefore, essential to compare the wraparound mortgage with other financing methods.

38

Veterans Administration Insured Home Loans

The Veterans Administrations housing program is not nearly as diversified as the HUD insured housing programs. The interest rate is the same as the FHA 203 (b) program. However, the VA does not require mortgage insurance premiums, like the FHA-insured program does. Therefore, the VA interest rate is slighter lower than that of FHA insured loans. The veteran's total eligibility is $27,500. Lenders, however, will make VA-insured loans of up to four times the eligibility. This means that the veteran is entitled to a $110,000 home loan. He must meet the home loan standards in order to qualify for a VA loan. If the veteran is unable to purchase a home with the maximum VA mortgage, he must find one that is within his financial capacity. Unlike the HUD 235 interest subsidy program, the VA does not subsidize any part of the interest! A veteran can reuse his eligibility providing he sells his VA-insured home. A veteran who has used his eligibility before and has sold the house with new financing and paid off the old VA loan may have his full VA entitlement renewed. However, if the veteran sells his home on an assumption and does not obtain new financing, even though he obtained a release of liability from the buyer, the veteran's eligibility will not be restored.

The Veterans Administration will allow the seller to pay all costs incurred in selling the property, including closing costs and prepaids. The veteran buyer can, therefore, purchase a home without spending any money.

A veteran can also have two open loans insured by VA. However, these two loans, combined must not exceed the total veteran eligibility. The advantage of buying a VA-insured home is that the homebuyer can save a substantial sum of money on the down payment. The mortgage payments on a VA-insured loan would be slightly higher for the same-price home insured by the FHA, because the buyer's mortgage would be higher. Although a veteran can purchase a home insured with a VA loan that cost up to $110,000, the buyer must meet the VA's home loan underwriting criteria before the loan is approved. The vet-

147

eran must have enough residual income to make the mortgage payments on the loan. Homebuyers should check with VA for recent changes in regulations. It is necessary however, for the veteran to occupy the new home. The seller is allowed to pay all costs, including closing costs; hence a veteran can buy and move into a new home without incurring any expenses.

The Veterans Administration's home loan underwriting standards are different from conventional and FHA home loan underwriting standards. The VA requires that the homebuyers' residual income exceeds the total housing expenses. Assume that a veteran buys a $65,500 home at 14 percent interest for thirty years. The mortgage payments would be $776. If other expenses included property taxes, $45; hazard insurance, $20; utilities, $125; and maintenance, $25; the total housing expenses would be $996. The following income and expense schedule is used to illustrate the effects that the homebuyer's income, debts, and residual income will have on his ability to meet the VA home loan underwriting standards. Assume that the homebuyer's net income is $2,575.

Income and Expense Schedule

Total Housing Expense		$996
Total Net Income		$2,575
Recurring Bills		
Installments Accounts	$150	
Two Auto Loans	$325	
Social Security	$145	
Allowances		
Two Adults ($200)	$400	
Three Teenagers ($150)	$450	
Total Expense		$1,470
Total *Residual* Income		$1,105

The above income and expense schedule shows that the homebuyer has $1,105 residual income after all expenses are deducted ($2,575 net income less $1,470 total expenses). In this case, the VA would approve the homebuyer for a VA loan, providing there are no serious credit deficiencies. Had the buyer been overextended financially, the VA would normally reject the application for a VA home loan.

Many veterans have the impression that they cannot get a VA-insured home loan if the old loan has not been paid in full. Even though the veteran has used his entitlement and sold his home to a buyer on an assumption, he may still have enough entitlement remaining to purchase another home. The following VA home loan entitlement schedule shows the amount of loan that a veteran may still obtain.

Veterans Administration Home Eligibility Entitlement Limits

Year	Entitlement Amount	Maximum Mortgage	Entitlement Remaining
1950	$7,500	$30,000	$80,000
1968	$12,500	$50,000	$60,000
1974	$17,500	$70,000	$40,000
1978	$25,000	$100,000	$10,000
1980	$27,500	$110,000	0

If the veteran has sold his home on an assumption, the amount of VA-insured loan that he is eligible for can be computed by using the following formula:

$$AVL = 4 \times (EVE - OVE)$$

For example, if a veteran purchased a home with a VA loan in 1965 when the maximum VA entitlement was $7,500, he could still obtain a $80,000 loan. This amount is computed by substituting the figures into the formula as follows:

SYMBOL DEFINITIONS

AVA—Amount of VA loan
EVE—Existing VA entitlement
OVE—Old VA entitlement
Amount of VA loan = 4 × $27,500 less $7,500
Amount of VA loan = 4 × $20,000
Amount of VA loan = $80,000

The veteran should always check the amount of his old VA entitlement to ascertain the amount of loan that VA would insure. The veteran may also add an amount to the remaining entitlement to increase the size of the loan. Effective March 1, 1986, the VA made the significant changes that will affect financially the veteran who is trying to purchase a home. The new regulations limit the amount of a VA-insured loan to $90,000. Veterans who have used their VA entitlement will not be eligible for another VA-insured loan. A veteran will no longer be able to refinance his home. This means that a veteran that has a high

149

interest loan will have to use a conventional mortgage loan if he wants to take advantage of low interest rate loans. In addition, the veteran will not be able to buy a larger home if part of his entitlement has been used. These changes may be modified at some future date; however, they will eliminate many veterans from the housing market.

VETERANS ADMINISTRATION PREQUALIFICATION TEST

The Veterans Administration uses analytical techniques that are quite different from conventional and FHA techniques to determine if the homebuyer is financially capable of making mortgage payments. FHA and conventional financing are based upon percentages of the homebuyer's income, while the VA looks at the residual income that is available to make the mortgage payments after all expenses have been paid.

VETERANS ADMINISTRATION MORTGAGE CRITERIA

GROSS INCOME
Salary _____
Overtime _____
Commission _____
Co-Mortgagor Income _____
Total Income _____
DEDUCTIONS FROM INCOME
Federal Income Tax _____
State Tax _____
    Net Income _____

To meet Veterans Administration home loan standards, the total residual income must exceed the total housing expenses. The homebuyer will be rejected if his residual income is less than the total housing expenses.

PROJECTED HOUSING
EXPENSE
Principal and Interest _____
Insurance _____
Property Taxes _____
Maintenance _____
Utilities _____
Total Housing Expenses _____
RESIDUAL INCOME
Net Income _____
DEDUCTIONS
Recurring Bills _____
Social Security _____
ALLOWANCE
Single Adults ($300) _____
Married Couple ($400) _____
Children ($150) _____
Total Deductions _____
    Residual Income _____

39

The HUD 203(b) Housing Program

The HUD Section 203(b) housing program is one of HUD's basic housing programs. This program was launched to enable homebuyers to purchase a home without paying an exorbitant amount for a down payment. Since the interest on HUD's Section 203(b) housing program is normally lower than conventional rates, the homebuyers pay less interest for financing the home. Consequently, the monthly mortgage payment would be smaller than that with a similar conventional mortgage.

The Section 203(b) housing program is a thirty-year, fixed-rate mortgage. The interest is not subsidized by the government. The buyers pay whatever the market interest rate is at the time of purchase. The housing and Urban Development Department does not loan money to the homebuyers; it insures the lenders who actually make the loans. In case the borrowers default on the loan, HUD pays the lender the total amount due under the mortgage note. HUD created the mortgage insurance premium program, which is a form of insurance that protects HUD and the lender against losses due to homebuyers' defaulting on mortgage loans. The homebuyer pays this charge to the lender, which provides a reserve fund for HUD. This charge is about one-half of 1 percent and is paid on a monthly basis with the mortgage payment. The FHA 203(b) program is the Housing and Urban Development standard mortgage program. It has enabled homebuyers to purchase homes without having to pay large sums of money for down payments. It also provided the opportunity to thousands of buyers who could not qualify for the higher conventional interest rates. Because of the constant change in the average price of a home, HUD makes periodic adjustments in the maximum sales price and mortgage amounts. In areas where the average price of a home exceeds the national norm, HUD generally will increase the mortgage amount that it will insure.

To qualify for a HUD-insured home loan, prospective homebuyers must meet HUD's home loan underwriting standards. The homebuyers must have a good credit rating. Any credit deficiencies such as outstanding collection accounts, judgments, tax liens, charge-offs, or slow credit must be corrected. The credit deficiencies must be justified. For example, if Harris was laid off from work because of a slowdown in business and, as a result, his account with a department store was sent to a collection agency for collection, a letter could be obtained from his employer showing that Harris's layoff caused a reduction or loss of income. Hence it can be construed that the credit deficiency was caused by conditions beyond his control. Another condition that contributes to credit deficiency is long-term illness that forces the homebuyer into temporary unemployment, causing a substantial reduction in income. Credit deficiencies caused by long-term illnesses or accidents can be documented by medical reports and letters from the homebuyer's employer.

Homebuyers are also required to meet HUD's established housing expense and debt-income ratio. The total housing expenses cannot exceed 35 percent of the homebuyer's net income. "Net income" is defined by HUD as the amount remaining after deducting federal income taxes. The housing expenses include the following: (1) mortgage payment, which is comprised of the principal and interest; (2) mortgage insurance premium; (3) hazard insurance; (4) property taxes; (5) utilities; (6) maintenance; and (7) homeowners association assessments (condominiums). Assume that Harris has a net income of $2,250 per month. Using the HUD housing expense ratio, Harris's total housing expenses could not exceed $788 ($2,250 net income × .35). Harris signed a contract to purchase a $55,500 home. He paid $4,000 as a down payment, leaving $51,500 to be financed with a thirty-year, 12 percent HUD-insured loan. The mortgage payment on the loan would be $530 principal and interest. If other housing expenses were: property taxes, $35; hazard insurance, $15; mortgage insurance, $15; maintenance, $25; and utilities, $125; the total housing expense would be $744. In order for Harris to qualify for the mortgage, 35 percent of Harris's income must equal or exceed $744. Since 35 percent of Harris's income is $788, he would meet HUD's housing expense ratio.

The other expense ratio that HUD uses to determine the financial capacity of the homebuyer to maintain the mortgage is the total recurring expenses ratio. These expenses are comprised of the total housing expenses plus debts requiring ten months or more to pay off. For example, if Harris's monthly debts that exceeded ten months included two auto loans ($175 on Auto A, $170 on Auto B) and other installment loans totalling $190, Harris' total monthly expense would be $1,279. The homebuyer total recurring monthly expenses cannot exceed 50 percent of his net monthly income. In Harris's case, his total recurring expenses could not exceed $1,125 ($2,250 monthly net income × .50, HUD-established recurring expenses ratio). Harris's total recurring expenses are $1,279, which is $154 more than the HUD 50 percent ratio. Unless Harris has favorable compensating factors, his application for a HUD-insured loan will be rejected even though he meets the HUD's 35 percent housing expense ratio. Harris could reduce his total recurring expenses ratio to meet HUD's 50 percent guideline by selling either one of the autos or by reducing his installment accounts by $144. If Harris has favorable compensating factors that would, in effect, reduce HUD's insurance risk, he may be approved for a home loan. The following conditions represent favorable compensating factors that HUD may consider in analyzing homebuyers' loan applications: (1) Substantial reserves for contingencies (saving accounts); (2) No automobile, (3) benefits not included in net income but that affect positively financial ability to pay (For example, automobile provided for the homebuyer's personal use by his employer); (4) temporary income that may affect the financial capacity of the homebuyer to pay short-term nonrecurring expenses. Other factors may be considered when they reduce the insurance risks of HUD in a given case. The amount of the down payment under the HUD 203(b) program is computed by taking 3 percent of the first $25,000 and 5 percent of the balance. For example, the down payment on a home costing $75,500 would be $3,275 (.03 × $25,000 + .05 × $50,500). If the down payment under a conventional mortgage was 10 percent, the buyer would save $4,225 ($7,500 conventional down payment less $3,275 HUD down payment).

40

The HUD Graduated Payment Mortgage (GPM 245)

The increase in the cost of buying a home has forced many Americans out of the housing market. The dream of owing a home is turning into an impossible wish as more families are being rejected for loans because of a lack of financial capacity. The perpetual rise in the cost of housing has caused lenders to develop many different kinds of mortgages and other kinds of innovative real estate financing plans. These mortgages and plans are designed to change the homebuyer's income structure to enable him to qualify for the home loan underwriting standards.

The HUD Graduated Payment Mortgage (GPM) housing program was obviously created to accommodate those families who could not qualify for traditional financing and whose incomes were too high for the HUD subsidized 235 housing program. It was a program in which HUD tried on an experimental basis to see if it would be successful in providing opportunties for prospective homebuyers who were being rejected for mortgages due to the escalating cost of housing. The experimental housing program was initiated in 1976. Information gathered by HUD showed that the program would meet housing needs of homebuyers falling within a specific income bracket. The program was modified, revisions were made, and, in 1977, it became a permanent housing program through the Housing and Community Development Act of 1977. Since the inception of the HUD Graduated Payment Mortgage, thousands of American families have realized their long sought dream of owning a home.

The GPM program is very similiar to the builder's interest buy-down programs. The key element that makes the program work is that the reduction in interest changes the housing expense and total debt income ratio, lowering them to accommodate the mortgage payments. The lower monthly mortgage payments reduce the ratios below the lender's and HUD's home mortgage underwriting standards. The significant differences between the developer's interest reduction plans and the HUD GPM plan are: (a) the developers submit a lump sum deposit to buy the interest down for a specified number of years; (b) under the GPM program, the homebuyers borrow additional money to buy the interest down; (c) the term of the buy-down period is shorter with a developer interest reduction plan; and (d) the homebuyer generally pays more in interest on a GPM program, due to the length of the interest reduction period. Under the GPM plan, the initial mortgage payment is lowered.

There are five different plans in which the mortgage payments increases from 2 percent to 7½ percent. The term of the plans is five or ten years. This means that should the homebuyer elect to participate in the GPM Plan II, the monthly mortgage payments will increase at the rate of 5 percent each year for five years. The less the percentage change in monthly payments and the longer the term of the increase, the lower the mortgage payment will be. To illustrate, the initial mortgage payment on a mortgage loan of $70,550 under the GPM Plan III with a 7½ percent increase in mortgage payment for five years would be approximately $681. The mortgage payment under the GPM Plan IV with a 2 percent increase for ten years would be $785. The homebuyer has an opportunity to review and analyze five different GPM plans, all of which have different mortgage payments. In essence, the prospective homebuyer has the opportunity to select a plan that is commensurate with his income structure. Although the home loan standards would automatically cause a homebuyer to purchase a home that is within his income capacity, he must make a realistic assessment of his financial growth to determine if there will be enough future income to compensate for the increase in monthly mortgage payments. Failure of the buyer's income to increase proportionally with the increase in mortgage payments could result in mortgage delinquency and default, where the lender has to foreclose on the buyer. Many unsuspecting homebuyers have lost their homes through foreclosure because of the growing disparity in income and the perpetual increase in mortgage payments under the GPM program.

The plan to select should be based on individual circumstances. For example, a homebuyer who anticipates regular substantial annual increases in his salary may prefer the GPM Plan III. This plan has the lowest mortgage payment, but the greatest increases, 7½ percent in mortgage payments. Those homebuyers whose incomes change less frequently or at a lower rate should consider the GPM Plan IV, where the mortgage payments start low and increase at a small 2 percent rate for ten years. To illustrate the financial impact that the GPM plan could have, assume that Hawkins and Lane purchased homes using the GPM mortgage for financing. They purchased similiar homes in the same subdivision. Hawkins used the GPM Plan II, with lower initial mortgage payments but high annual increases of 5 percent. Lane used the GPM Plan IV, with higher mortgage payments but at a 2 percent annual increase in mortgage payments. The amount of the down payment is determined by the type of GPM plan selected. In effect, this implies that even though the price of the homes may be the same, the amount of the mortgage loan will vary in accordance with the amount of the down payment. In the preceding example, the price of the homes purchased was $73,000 for thirty years at 13½ percent. Because of the two different plans, the mortgage loan amounts would be different. Hawkins's initial mortgage payment under the GPM plan would be approximately $611, while Lane's initial mortgage payment under the GPM Plan IV wold be approximately $726. At the end of the first year, Hawkins's mortgage payments would increase to $714, a $34 dollar increase. Lane's mortgage payments would increase to $742, a $15 dollar increase. The difference in the amounts of the down payment required under the different GPM programs caused the difference in the initial mortgage payments. The down payment under the GPM Plan III is higher than the down payment under the GPM Plan IV. This difference is due to the lower interest rate of Plan IV.

The following schedule contains approximations of the down payment on homes for thirty years at 14 percent interest.

Down Payment Approximation Schedule
Price of Home and Down Payment

Plan	$64,000	$70,000	$80,000
I	$2,600	$2,800	$3,350
II	$4,750	$5,200	$6,100
III	$6,750	$7,400	$8,550
IV	$4,500	$7,650	$5,750
V	$7,000	$8,850	$5,750

An examination of the above schedule shows that the GPM Plan I has the lowest down payment while Plan V requires the largest down payment. Under the GPM Plan IV, the mortgage payment would have the smallest annual increase.

The mortgage payment schedule below shows the differences in percentages and amounts of annual increases in mortgage payments on a $68,000 home after the required down payment under the GPM Plans for thirty years at 14 percent interest.

GPM Mortgage Payment Schedule

PLAN	PERCENT INCREASE	MORTGAGE PAYMENT	AMOUNT OF INCREASE
I	2½%	$739	$18.48
II	5%	$658	$33.90
III	7½%	$587	$44.03
IV	2%	$704	$14.08
V	3%	$641	$19.28

The schedule shows that the largest increase in mortgage is under the GPM Plan III. The increase is quite large, compared to those of other increasing mortgage programs. It is, therefore, important for the homebuyer to select a plan that will enable him to maintain financial control over his debts and income.

To illustrate how much the mortgage payment may increase, assume that Jones purchased a home, under the GPM Plan III, costing $68,000 at 14 percent for thirty years. The payment for the first year would be $587. It would increase at the rate of 7½ percent for five years. The total amount of the increase over five years would be approximately $2,362. The new mortgage payment at the end of the fifth year would be $840 ($587 initial mortgage payment + $253 total amount of increase in five years). This increase constitutes a 43 percent increase in mortgage payment. Unless the homebuyer's income increases at a proportionate rate, the homebuyer could be faced with imminent foreclosure because of his financial inability to maintain the mortgage.

41

Buying a Home Using the FHA 203(k) Housing Program

The FHA 203(k) Housing Program is not very well known. It, however, is one where a homebuyer can purchase an existing home that is within his financial capacity. HUD's purpose of the 203(k) program is to promote and facilitate the restoration and preservation of the nation's housing stock.

The 203(k) program provides the homebuyer an opportunity to buy and rehabilitate an existing home where the total mortgage amount may be substantially lower than the cost of new construction. It provides the homebuyer with enough funds to purchase and rehabilitate the home. The program enables the buyer to locate housing in established neighborhoods, thereby avoiding more expensive homes in outlying areas. The borrower must meet the same home loan standards discussed under the FHA 203(b) Housing Program. The maximum mortgage amount and down payment or loan-to-value is also the same as with the 203(b) program. The buyer must pay as a down payment 3 percent of the first $25,000 and 5 percent of the balance of the total amount of the cost of the house, plus the rehabilitation costs. Assume that Willis purchased a $45,500 home using the FHA 203(k) program. He calls in a contractor, who estimates the rehabilitation cost to be $7,500. The down payment on the home is $2,150 (.03 × $25,000 + .05 × $53,000, total cost of home including rehabilitation less $25,000). Similiar homes in the neighborhood are selling for $65,000.

The buyer should have a contractor estimate the cost of rehabilitation prior to making a decision to purchase the home. The total price of the home including the rehabilitation cost can be compared with the market values of similar homes. The buyer would also be able to accurately estimate the amount of equity that would be generated under the 203(k) Housing Program as compared to under traditional mortgage programs. The buyer must be careful of the condition of the home he plans to purchase. He should also be concerned about the condition of the neighborhood. Homes located in declining neighborhoods could conceivably, after the acquistion and rehabilitation costs, have a market value that is less than the total cost of the home.

The following comparison schedule shows the instant equity that would be accumulated in the home using the FHA 203(k) Housing Program:

Comparison Schedule

FHA 203(K) MORTGAGE		CONVENTIONAL MORTGAGE	
Sales Price of Home	$45,500	Sales Price of Home	$65,500
Rehabilitation Cost	7,500	Rehabilitation Cost	-0-
Total Cost of Home	$53,000	Total Cost of Home	$65,500
HUD Required Down		10 Percent Down	
Payment	2,150	Payment	6,660
Amount of Mortgage	$50,850	Amount of Mortgage	$58,950
Market Value of		Market Value of	
Home	$65,500	Home	$65,500
Amount of Mortgage	$50,850	Amount of Mortgage	$58,950
Buyer's Equity	$14,650	Buyer's Equity	$ 6,650

The comparison schedule shows that by selecting the proper home that does not require substantial rehabilitation, the homebuyer could generate twice as much equity under the 203(k) program than could be created with traditional mortgage financing. The mortgage amount could also be less using the 203(k) program. Normally, FHA's interest rate is 1 percent lower than conventional mortgage rates. Assume that the conventional interest rate is 14 percent; FHA interest rate would be 13 percent. The mortgage payment at the 14 percent conventional rate on the $58,950, thirty-year mortgage is $698, compared to $563 for 13 percent interest on the $50,850, thirty-year mortgage. The buyer could conceivably reduce the mortgage payment and the down payment by utilizing the 203(k) program.

The inspection and release schedule is an important part of the rehabilitation loan agreement. It is also a protective document that controls the amount of and the frequency of payments made to the contractor for completion of rehabilitation work. The HUD construction analyst uses the plans submitted by the contractor to determine the number of inspections that are needed to insure compliance with specifications, property standards, and materials. The analyst also monitors the schedule of payments. This document outlines the various repair stages of when payment will be made and the amount that will be paid the contractor for rehabilitation work that has been completed satisfactorily. If work is not performed as delineated in the work specifications or inferior materials are used, the analyst can cause payment to be withheld until corrections have been made.

The number of inspections is dependent upon the extent and the complexity of the rehabilitation work; therefore, it is important for the buyer to have an estimate done to ascertain the extent of repairs required to bring the home up to standards. The extent of the required rehabilitation work will also determine how long it will take the lender to close the transaction. If the rehabilitation work is excessive, requiring substantial electrical, plumbing, and structural repairs, the number of inspections and payment schedule for the work completed will be extended.

The lender is required to establish an interest-bearing escrow account, the money of which is deposited and reserved for rehabilitation of the home purchased by the buyer. The lender releases funds to the contractor upon completion of specific phases of work as outlined in the inspection and release schedule. The contractor must submit a compliance inspection to the lender. This report certifies that the work has been completed in compliance with the work specifications. This report protects the homebuyer against poor workmanship and assures him that quality materials are used to rehabilitate the home. If the work has not been completed in accordance with specifications, the contractor will not be paid until the work meets the standards.

Homebuyers who desire to live in established neighborhoods where taxes are stabilized and other neighborhood amenities, such as churches, shopping facilities, and child-care and medical facilities, are already in existance. Those homebuyers who cannot afford to buy newly constructed homes that are located in surburban areas may be able to find homes that they can purchase and rehabilitate and are within their financial limitations.

42

Using the FHA 235 Interest Subsidized Housing Program to Purchase a Home

The Housing and Urban Development 235 Interest Subsidy Housing Program has allowed many Americans the opportunity to buy homes. Many of these families would never have the opportunity of buying homes under traditional financing methods. The FHA 235 subsidy program has been modified many times. It operates by the government subsidizing a percentage of the interest. The effect of the subsidy reduces the overall mortgage payments to enable homebuyers to meet the home loan underwriting criteria. The 235 interest subsidy program is capable of assisting homebuyers to qualify for homes that they could not purchase using other financing methods, such as the ARM and the interest buy-down plans.

Homebuyers, to qualify, must fall within HUD-established income limitations. The income may vary in each of the HUD regions. The income limits would be higher in high-cost areas and lower in lower-cost areas. Income limitations for the FHA 235 interest subsidy program can be obtained from the local FHA office. The income eligibility requirement is based upon family adjusted income. This income is determined by including income from all sources that the family anticipates receiving for the next 12 months. Adjustments are made for Social Security. A deduction of $300 is allowed for each minor child. Some incomes that may be excluded are unusual or temporary income and income earned by minors.

To illustrate how adjusted income is determined, assume that Adams is purchasing a home under the FHA subsidy housing program. His annual gross income is $22,400. He has three teenage children. Two of the children work part-time after school. Both of the teenagers work twenty hours per week, each earning four dollars per hour. If the Social Security is 7 percent, Adams's adjusted income could be calculated by dividing his annual gross income by twelve months ($22,400 gross income divided by 12 months) and deducting the other allowances. Income earned by the minor children is not included. Assume that the amount of the Social Security is $137. Since Adams has three children, the total allowance would be $900, based on a deduction of $300 per minor child. The income earned by the minor children is not included in the adjusted income calculation. The following schedule shows the adjusted income after eligible allowances have been deducted:

Adjusted Income Schedule

Gross Annual Income		$22,400
ELIGIBLE DEDUCTIONS		
Allowance for Children	$900	
Social Security	$137	
Total Deductions		$1,037
Adjusted Annual Income		$21,363

The adjusted monthly income is $1,780 ($21,363 adjusted annual income divided by 12). This is the income that will be used to determine if Adams falls within the 235 income limitations. To illustrate how the subsidy program operates, assume that HUD is subsidizing down to 6 percent from the market rate of 14½ percent. Adams is buying a $65,500 home. He paid the closing cost and a $3,500 down payment. HUD uses two formulas to compute the amount of subsidy or assistance payment that will be applied to reduce the interest on the mortgage. The first assistance payment formula is the difference between total monthly payment, including principal, interest at market rate, MIP (Mortgage Insurance Premium), property taxes, hazard insurance, and 20 percent of the homebuyer's adjusted monthly income. Assume that HUD will subsidize the interest down to 6 percent. The Assistance Payment (AP) under the second formula is the difference between monthly mortgage payment, including principal, interest (at market rate), and MIP and the mortgage payment under the HUD 6 percent subsidy. The HUD interest subsidy changes on a periodic basis to compensate for changes in market rate interest.

Assume that the market interest rate is 14½ percent. The HUD Assistance Payment Formula One would be: AP = PI + PT + HI + MIP less .20 (AI). Since Adams paid $3,500 down, the amount of the mortgage would be $62,000 ($65,500 price of home less $3,500 down payment). The monthly mortgage payment on a $62,000 mortgage for 30 years at 14½ percent interest would be $760. If other expenses included property tax, $35; hazard insurance, $20; and MIP, $24; the total mortgage payment at market rate is $839. Twenty percent of Adams' adjusted income is $356 (.20 × $1,780). Substituting these figures in the HUD Assistance Payment Formula One ($760 + $35 + $20 + $24 less $356, 20 percent of Adams's adjusted income), the amount of the assistance payment would be $483. Using the HUD Formula Two, AP = P&I (market rate interest) + MIP less P&I (at HUD 6 percent subsidy), and substituting the figures ($760 + $24 less $412 HUD 6 percent interest subsidy), the assistance payment is $372. The amount of the assistance payment under the HUD 235 interest subsidy program would be the lesser of the two amounts. Since the Formula Two amount is smaller than that of Formula One, the amount of the HUD subsidy would be $372. Adams's share of the mortgage payment is $467 ($839, total mortgage payment, less $372, HUD's assistance payment). In addition to meeting the HUD's 235 subsidy eligibility guidelines, Adams must also qualify for the HUD home loan underwriting standards established for other housing programs. Adams's total housing expense cannot exceed 35 percent of his monthly net income. His total recurring bills cannot exceed 50 percent of his net income. Under HUD's homebuying guidelines, net income is the gross income less income tax. If Adams pays $150 per month for income taxes, his net income would be $1,950 gross income less $150 income taxes, $1,800. Assume that utilities are estimated to be $165; maintenance, $125; and recurring bills, $215 per month. The following home loan eligibility percentage schedule compares Adams's debt-income ratio with the home loan percentage ratios required to meet HUD's home underwriting standards:

Home Loan Eligibility Percentage Ratio Schedule

	HUD Guideline	Actual Amount	Amount Over/Under
Housing Expense	$630	$657	$27
Recurring Bills	$900	$872	$28

The schedule shows that Adams's housing expenses are $27 over the 35 percent allowed by HUD guidelines. His total monthly recurring bill is twenty-eight dollars under the maximum amount allowed by HUD's recurring expense ratio. If Adams had very good credit and had established a history of credit reliability, HUD would consider his good credit as a favorable compensatory factor and approve the home loan.

The homebuyer income is recertified annually. The purpose of the recertification is to insure that the amount of the assistance paid on behalf of the homebuyer reflects a reasonable and actual need of the homebuyer for financial assistance. If the income should increase, the HUD subsidy would be reduced. If the homebuyer's income should decrease, the HUD subsidy would increase to compensate for the change. If the homebuyer's income should increase to the extent that recertification computation shows that the homebuyer could afford to pay market rate interest, the HUD assistance payments would be terminated. An example would be where a family qualified for the subsidy program based only on the father's income. Should the mother obtain permanent employment, the family's combined income may exceed HUD's income limitations. Many homebuyers have lost their HUD assistance payments because of substantial increases in their income.

A percentage of the subsidy is recaptured by HUD upon the occurrence of the following conditions: (A) upon the sale of the property to a homebuyer not qualified to receive assistance payments, and (B) when the homebuyer rents the home for more than one year. The amount of the subsidy that must be repaid by the homeowner will be the lesser of the actually amount paid by HUD or 50 percent of the net appreciation of the property. Net appreciation is the amount of the increase in value of the property less cost of selling the home and cost of improvements made to the property. To illustrate, suppose that Adams added a new fireplace that cost $1,500 and a block fence that cost $2,500. After five years, Adams decided to sell the home and move to another state. The home had an appreciated value of $85,500. Adams paid a 5 percent sales commission to a real estate agency to sell the home. The amount of the sales commssion was $4,275, determined by the following calculation ($85,500 value of home × 05 percent sales commission). The amount of the assistance paid by HUD after making adjustments for salary changes was $9,300. The amount that must be repaid by the homeowner would be the lesser of the $9,300 amount of assistnce paid by HUD and 50 percent of the net appreciated value of the property. After five years, the home had an appreciated value of $85,500; therefore, the appreciated amount is $20,000, ($85,500 less $65,500 purchase price of the home). The amount of the NET appreciation is $11,725, ($20,000 amount appreciated in value less $8,275 total amount of deductions for improvements plus selling costs). Fifty percent of the net appreciated value of the home is $5,863 ($11,725, net appreciated amount, × .50, recapture percentage). The amount that the homeowner must reimburse HUD is $5,863. This amount is less than the $9,300 assistance payment that was paid by HUD.

The HUD 235 Subsidized Housing Program is a very costly program. The government has modified the program many times to reduce the operating cost. The recapture provision has enabled the government to recoup some of the expense of operating the program. There will probably be other modifications and changes, such as decreasing the income limitations to limit the number of homebuyers who would be eligible to participate in the subsidy program. One of the major advantages of the 235 program is that homebuyers with substantially lower incomes can purchase homes with mortgage payments that would be within their income capacity. The program has made home ownership available to thousands of families who would never be able to qualify for traditional mortgages.

Eligibility Determination
for
Home Ownership Assistance under
FHA Section 235

A. Computation of Annual Family Income
  1. Total Annual Adult Income ....$_____
  2. Less 7% (Social Security) ....$_____
  3. Adjusted Annual Income ....$_____
  4. Less Number of Minors × $300 ....$_____
  5. Adjusted Annual Family Income ....$_____
  6. Adjusted Monthly Income (A-5 divided by 12 months)$_____

B. Assistance Calculations Formula One
  1. Monthly Mortgage Payments
    (Principal, Interest at Market Rate, MIP, Taxes, Insurance) ....$_____
  2. 20% of Adjusted Monthly Income (A-6) ....$_____
  3. Formula (1) Assistance Payment (B-1 Less B-2) ....$_____

C. Assistance Calculations Formula Two
  1. Monthly Mortgage Payment
    (Principal, Interest, and MIP at Market Rate) ....$_____
  2. Mortgage Payment (Principal and Interest at 5%) ......$_____
  3. Formula Two Assistance Payment (C-1 Less C-2) ....$_____

D. Homebuyer Mortgage Payment Calculation
  1. Mortgage Payment (B-1) ....$_____
  2. HUD Assistance Payment
    (Lesser of Formula One and Formula Two) ....$_____
  3. Homebuyer Mortgage Payment under the Subsidy
    (Lesser of Formula One and Formula Two ....$_____

43

Using the Pledge Account Mortgage (PAM) to Finance a Home

The real estate industry has developed many different ways of financing homes. Many of these financing techniques are designed for developers, such as the interest reduction plans and the Adjusted Rate Mortgages. Those homebuyers who wanted to buy homes with a below market interest mortgage were unable to qualify until the Adjusted Rate Mortgage and the Pledge Account Mortgage (PAM) were designed. Prior to development of these two mortgages, homebuyers who wanted to buy existing homes had to use the traditional market rate mortgages. Because of the lack of financial versatility, many homebuyers could not purchase homes because they could not meet the home loan underwriting criteria. When the Pledge Account Mortgage (PAM) came on the real estate financing scene, many of those homebuyers who could not qualify to purchase homes because of a lack of income were able to buy homes using the Pledge Account Mortgage.

The PAM is similiar to the builder's or developer's buy-down plans. There are, however, several significant differences. First, the developer's or builder's buy-down is designed for new constructions. Homebuyers have to buy homes in the developer's subdivisions. With a Pledge Account Mortgage, the homebuyer could purchase new or existing homes in virtually any area, providing he has the income capacity. Like the builder's interest buy-down plans, the Pledge Account Mortgage requires that a specified amount be put into a special reserve account to buy the interest down, which, in effect, reduces it below market rate. Second, under the builder's buy-down or interest reduction plans, the builders put up the money to buy the interest down up to 3 percent and more. However, there are some developers with extremely attractive interest buy-down plans of 5 and 6 percent. One disadvantage of the builder's buy down plan is that the builders are normally able to recover the cost of the buy-down by inflating the sales price of the home. Under the Pledge Account Mortgage, the buyer's relatives or friends can buy the interest down.

The Pledge Account Mortgage can make a significant difference in determining how much of a mortgage the homebuyer can afford. Many homebuyers may have accumulated the down payment. They may have worked diligently to save enough money for the down payment, or they may have sold their home in order to buy a larger home in a more prestigious neighborhood. The income criteria is what prevents most homebuyers from qualifying for new home loans. Assume that Watkins sold his home in order to buy a home in Blue Haven Estate, a prestigious surburban neighborhood. Watkins is interested in purchasing a home that costs $110,500. After paying off the existing mortgage, Watkins received $40,500 for his equity. He wants to retain $8,500 to buy new furniture for the new home. This would leave $32,000 to pay down on the new home. If Watkins paid the $32,000 down on the new home, he would have to get a $78,500 mortgage to finance the home. Watkins has a gross monthly income of $2,900. If the lender uses a 30 percent housing expense ratio, Watkins could afford only $870 for housing expense, computed by using the calculation (.30 × $2,900 gross monthly income). The mortgage payment on a $78,500 mortgage at 14½ percent interest for 30 years is $960 per month. If the expenses on the new home were, property taxes $40, hazard insurance $30, and mortgage insurance $25, the total amount of the monthly housing expense would be $1,055. Since Watkins can afford only $870 for housing expense, the lender would reject his application for a home mortgage loan. The Pledge Account Mortgage would have the effect of reducing the interest rate. Now suppose that Watkins's father decided to use a Pledge Account Mortgage to buy the interest down to 10½ percent to help Watkins meet the lender's underwriting standards. The mortgage payment on a $78,500 mortgage for thirty years at 10½ percent is $718 per month, principle and interest. The total housing expense, using the Pledge Account Mortgage, would be $813. Since Watkins could afford a housing expense of $870 per month, by using the Pledge Account Mortgage to finance the home, he would need only $2,710 gross monthly income to qualify. Watkins's gross income is $2,900.

One significant advantage that the Pledge Account Mortgage has over the Adjusted Rate Mortgages (ARM) is that under the Pledge Account Mortgage, the interest stabilizes after the interest reduction adjustment period ends. In the preceding example, under the PAM, at the end of the three-year adjustment period, the mortgage payment, principal, and interest would be approximately $952. The mortgage payment on an Adjusted Rate Mortgage could be much higher. Assume that the inflation rate caused the interest rate to reach 16½ percent at the end of the three years, with a 3 percent increase for each the second and third year. The mortgage payments would be approximately $1,084 per month, compared to $952 under the Pledge Account Mortgage. The difference constitutes a $132 increase in mortgage payment. It is, therefore, essential that the homebuyer be aware of the effect that the Pledge Account Mortgage will have on the increase in mortgage payments compared to other mortgages. One of the most essential disadvantages of the PAM compared to the conventional thirty-year fixed-rate mortgage is the condition called mortgage payment shock. Under the preceding example, the mortgage payment at the end of the adjustment period would be $952, compared to $718 per month during the three-year PAM interest reduction period.

The Pledge Account Mortgage will work very well for those homebuyers who anticipate annual increases in their income that will offset the increases in mortgage payment after the PAM interest adjustment period ends. Under the Pledge Account Mortgage, if the buyer puts up the money to buy the interest down, he could use the interest to reduce income taxes. However, under the interest reduction plan where the developer puts up the money to buy the interest down, the homebuyer could not deduct the interest from his income as a tax shelter.

44

Conducting Housing Inspections

Buying a house is similar to buying a car. As with a car, you should know the condition of the house before signing a sales agreement. New homes as well as older homes may have defects not visible to a person not accustomed to inspecting homes. Hence it is very important for the buyer to make a complete and thorough inspection of the home. This could save the buyer hundreds of dollars by uncovering defects and having the seller make the corrections as a condition of the sales agreement. If the buyer feels inadequate in conducting the inspection, a professional home inspector could be consulted and contracted to make the inspection. The inspector would submit a detailed report depicting the conditions of the home.

A checklist comparable to the following should be used to determine the condition of the home.

Inspection Checklist

EXTERIOR OF HOME	POOR	FAIR	GOOD
1. Foundation: Look for freedom from cracks and/or settling.			
2. Masonry: Notice loose mortar, cracks, and/or missing bricks.			
3. Siding: Check for loose, warped, and/or missing pieces.			
4. Exterior Paint: Notice fading and/or peeling.			
5. Windows: Examine for broken, or missing, screens, cracked panels, warping, torn screens.			

6. Roof: Check for excessive weathering, missing or damaged shingles, age. _____ _____ _____
7. Gutters and downspouts: Look for missing sections, corrosion, and loose joints. _____ _____ _____
8. Chimney: Check loose flashing and tilting. _____ _____ _____
9. Walls and fences: Check foundation and tilting. _____ _____ _____
10. Sidewalk and driveway: Look for settling and cracks. _____ _____ _____
11. Sewage disposal system: Check location, capacity, and drainage of septic tank. _____ _____ _____
12. Landscaping: Look for poor drainage; condition of shrubs and trees. _____ _____ _____
13. Garage: Check doors, roof, siding, and windows. _____ _____ _____

INTERIOR OF HOME

1. Structure of home: Check for sagging. _____ _____ _____
2. Floors: Look for cracks on floors, loose boards. _____ _____ _____
3. Stairs: Inspect handrails; look for loose treads. _____ _____ _____
4. Plumbing Systems _____ _____ _____
   A. Water pipes: Check for leaks and/or corrosion. _____ _____ _____
   B. Toilets: Check flushing and leakage. _____ _____ _____
   C. Hot Water Heater: Inspect for signs of rusting and leakage, capacity. _____ _____ _____
   D. Heating: Inspect type of heating and note cost to operate. _____ _____ _____
   E. Cooling and Refrigeration: Check for age, and operating

expense, and if unit is under
warranty. _____ _____ _____
  F. Water Pressure: Note
adequacy. _____ _____ _____
  G. Sinks: Check for proper
drainage and leakage.
  5. Electrical: Check age, type fuse or
circuit breaker, voltage number,
and size of circuit. _____ _____ _____
  6. Kitchen and Appliances _____ _____ _____
  A. Range and Oven: Inspect
condition; note age. _____ _____ _____
  B. Refrigerator _____ _____ _____
  C. Dishwasher: Check operation. _____ _____ _____
  D. Disposal: Look for leakage. _____ _____ _____
  E. Cabinets: Inspect doors and
finish. _____ _____ _____
  F. Floor: Look for missing tiles
and/or cracked, warping wood
floors. _____ _____ _____
  7. Living Room: Note adequate size
and whether there is a fireplace. _____ _____ _____
  8. Bedrooms: Note adequate size and
ample closet space. _____ _____ _____
  9. Bathroom: Check number,
ventilation, and size. _____ _____ _____
10. Walls and Ceilings: Check
sagging, falling acoustic tile or
plaster, and/or leakage. _____ _____ _____
11. Doors: Make sure they close
properly; check locks and
jamming. _____ _____ _____
12. Attics and basements: Check for
leakage, insulation and termite
damage. _____ _____ _____
13. Light Fixtures: Look for missing
covers, and/or defective switches. _____ _____ _____
14. Swimming Pool: Check for cracks,
operating condition of pumps,
light filter, timer, and aerators. _____ _____ _____

45

No–Down-Payment Sales
May Have Adverse Financial Impact
on Buyers and Sellers

One of the most important objectives of American citizens is to buy and own a home. In fact, it is the fervor behind this objective that has caused the proliferation of real estate "No Money Down Seminars." Those buyers who are looking to buy a home with no money down normally have to spend endless hours to locate such bargain sales. In many cases, when they do find a seller that is willing to participate in a no-money-down real estate sales transaction, terms have to be developed that could create financial hardships for both the buyer and seller. Many buyers have purchased homes with no money down; however, the financial arrangements have caused many of the buyers financial problems. Sponsors of no-money-down real estate seminars emphasized that a buyer can purchase a home even though the buyer has no job, no money, and lacks a satisfactory credit rating. The veracity of this contention can be confirmed by the many real estate sales transactions that have been consummated by buyers who purchased homes without a down payment.

Purchasing a home with no money down requires close scrutiny of the language used in the contract. Both the buyer and seller should be completely cognizant of the arrangements and repercussions that may develop as a result of the buyer defaulting on the terms of the agreement. Two essential things must be considered by the buyer and seller when arranging a no-money-down sale transaction to buy property. First, the buyer should have a definite purpose in mind when a decision is made to buy property. Second, the buyer should make a realistic financial assessment of the projection of his income. In addition, the buyer should make an accurate assessment of the rentability and marketability of the home if it is being purchased for investment purposes. Failure to make an accurate and realistic projection of incomes and assessment of the rental market could cause the buyer to default on the mortgage note. This condition would result if the buyer's

172

income becomes inadequate to sustain the mortgage or the rental market demand decreases. Inadequate income has been the major contributor to mortgage delinquency and foreclosure. It is therefore of paramount importance for the buyer to purchase properties that are within his projected limitations.

IMPACT OF INADEQUATE INCOME PROJECTION

Real estate seminars suggest that buyers purchase homes with no money down, even if they have no income and no job. If the buyer purchases a home without conducting a realistic assessment of his projected income, he could be faced with a financial problem that could seriously damage both his and the seller's credit status. Damaged credit could affect their ability to arrange future credit transactions. Hence credit deficiencies that result from no-money-down real estate transactions may remain on the credit record for five or more years. In addition, if a balloon contract is involved in the transaction, the seller may obtain a judgment against the buyer that could prevent him from establishing credit.

The effect that an unrealistic assessment of future income could have on both the buyer and seller is depicted in the following illustration. Assume that a buyer locates a motivated seller, one who has to sell because his employer is relocating to another state. The buyer has no job and is collecting unemployment benefits. The buyer was recently laid off because of a substantial slowdown in business. The seller checked the buyer's credit status and found the the buyer was financially responsible. Because of his unfortunate conditions and circumstances, he decided to enter into an agreement with the buyer to sell the property for $72,500. The seller had an outstanding $47,500 mortgage. The terms of the contract required the seller to take out a $20,000 second mortgage and give the buyer a $5,000 two-year balloon contract with no monthly payments. The full amount of the $5,000 was due and payable in two years, including 10 percent interest. The terms of the balloon contract allowed the seller to demand payment in full if the home was sold before the due date of the contract. It also became due and payable if the buyer became delinquent with the first and second mortgage. The mortgage payment on the second mortgage at 14½ percent for fifteen years is $273. The total mortgage payment is $623. The buyer's unemployment benefits are $550 per month. However, the buyer is optimistic about obtaining employment within thirty days. The buyer moved into the home and was unable to make the first mortgage payment, because he could not find employment. The second mortgage company initiated foreclosure proceedings, because the buyer failed to make the mortgage payments according to the terms of the mortgage note. This condition evolved because the buyer did not make an accurate assessment of his future income.

The preceding situation could have an adverse impact on both the seller and the buyer. Since the buyer took out the second mortgage in his name, his credit will be seriously damaged as a result of the buyer defaulting on the mortgage. The seller, however, may also lose the $5,000 due him on the balloon contract. Since the buyer paid absolutely nothing down, there may not be a dedicated commitment by the buyer to repay the $5,000 balloon contract. In essence, the seller does not have a motivated buyer, because the buyer has nothing to lose except a good credit status.

A lack of substantial interest in the home by the buyer invariably relegates the seller to a precarious financial situation. The buyer has virtually no equity in the home; therefore, the seller has no security.

The down payment required by the Housing and Urban Development Department and conventional lenders is designed to create a commitment on the part of the buyer to protect his equity. A buyer who pays $10,000 down on a home has much more to lose than a buyer who purchases a home with no down payment. To prevent buyers from buying homes with no down payment, lenders used acceleration clauses or due-on-sale clauses that force the buyer to replace the existing mortgage with a new mortgage. The due-on-sale clause, hence, allows the mortgage lender to establish credit and financial standards for the buyer to protect his interest in the homes that are financed. It also puts the buyer in a situation where he would lose a substantial sum of money if he buys the home and subsequently defaults on the mortgage note.

FOUR BASIC REASONS WHY BUYERS PURCHASE HOMES

The American dream is to buy and own a home. However many buyers purchase homes for four basic reasons. Homeownership for many buyers provides relief from the responsibilities and restrictions of renting, while others have financial motives for buying homes. Buyers fall into the four following classifications: (1) For occupancy: The buyers intend to move into the home and enjoy all the ammenities of homeownership. (2) Investment: The buyer usually intends to hold the property for a specified period of time. When the market value of the property increases, the seller sells it for a profit. (3) Tax Shelter: The buyer's plan is to use the depreciation, interest, and maintenance to shelter his income and reduce his taxable income. (4) Income: This perhaps is often combined with either the tax shelter or investment purpose. In many cases, a buyer may buy a home for all the preceding reasons.

BUYING A HOME FOR INVESTMENT

Before a buyer purchases a home for investment, he should make an analysis of several essential factors. First, the buyer should be certain that the type of financial arrangements made will not cause the mortgage payment to exceed the market rate rents. This can be achieved by buying the property below the market price. Second, the buyer should make certain that the home is in a marketable area, both for resale and for renting purposes.

The following situation will delineate the importance of purchasing a home below market price. To illustrate, assume that a buyer desires to buy a home for investment. The market price of the home is $65,800. The seller has an existing $40,300 with monthly mortgage payments of $320. The buyer arranges to purchase the home for $50,800 with a fifteen-year 14 percent second mortgage.

The following schedule compares the financial differences of buying the home at market price and $15,000 below market price.

Market Comparison Schedule

	Market Price of Home	Below Market Price
Purchase Price of Home	$65,800	$50,800
Existing Mortgage on Home	$40,300	$40,300
Amount of Second Mortgage Required	$25,500	$10,500
Mortgage Payment on Second Mortgage	$340	$140
Mortgage Payment on First Mortgage	$320	$320
Total Mortgage Payment	$660	$460
Market Rate Rent	$575	$575
Rent Surplus or Shortage	$-85	$+115

The above schedule shows that if the buyer purchased the home at the market price, he would have a negative cash flow of eighty-five dollars per month. However, if he purchased the home below the market price, there would be a $115 positive cash flow. Many factors should be considered when the buyer decides to purchase property for investment. The preceding illustration is hypothetical. Actual figures may change in accordance with circumstances. The three most critical factors include (1) The purchase price of the home: This will determine the rental rates that the buyer must establish in order to meet the mortgage debt service level or mortgage obligation; (2) The type of financial arrangements or terms of the sale; (3) The resale and rental marketability of the property. This is perhaps the most important aspect of the investment. If the home cannot be resold or rented to make the mortgage payment on the loan or loans, the buyer may be stuck with property that could be vandalized if allowed to remain vacant. Hence the financial loss due to vandalism of the property would negate the purpose of the intended investment.

46

Twenty-five Things to Avoid When Buying a Home

Owning a home has always and will continue to be the American dream. Thousands of Americans realize their dream each month as they consummate real estate transactions. Many of these homebuyers are so obsessed with the idea of owning a home that they fail to use good judgement in making the largest purchase of their life. Poor judgment in buying a home has been extremely costly to homebuyers in terms of legal expense and home repairs. These expenses could have been avoided had the buyer been cognizant of the essential things to avoid when purchasing a home. By scrutinizing certain conditions and information, the homebuyer could avoid the costly mistakes that many homebuyers make in purchasing their homes. The following list of things to avoid can be used to avert legal and costly home repairs. The list covers the major things to avoid and is not represented to be a panacea or substitute for a complete housing inspection and advice from a competent real estate attorney:

1. AVOID: Allowing a real estate sales agent to talk you into buying a home that is not compatible with your financial capacity. Excessive financial obligations are the leading cause of foreclosure.
2. AVOID: Purchasing a home because of cosmetic improvements such as fancy wallpaper and/or decorative light fixtures. These add little value to the market value of the home. Other more important factors should be included when selecting a home.
3. AVOID: Buying a home using a land sales contract for financing. This is by far the most hazardous way of buying a home. Usually, the buyer is required to pay a third of the selling price and more before title is conveyed.
4. AVOID: Purchasing a home in a neighborhood where the appreciation of the homes is less than 3 percent per year. A slow appreciation rate causes the equity to grow at less than the normal rate; hence any major repairs may absorb the investment in the home.

5. AVOID: Buying a home without investigating the integrity and the real estate practices of the agency. By negotiating with dedicated and honest real estate agents, the homebuyer can avoid real estate transactions that may result in costly legal expense.

6. AVOID: Buying a home when the housing expense, principal, interest, insurance, and property tax exceed 30 percent of the homebuyer's gross monthly income. High housing expense ratios lead to mortgage delinquency and eventually foreclosure and should invariably be avoided.

7. AVOID: Purchasing a home without first having a title search completed to uncover any possible title defects. Encumbrances against the property can be very costly. It is therefore imperative to uncover these defects in the real estate negotiation so that proper corrective actions can be taken to remove the defects prior to the conveyance of title.

8. AVOID: Purchasing a home where there is no competent real estate attorney or real estate agent present to elaborate and interpret the effects of real estate terms, language, and contingencies. Improperly written real estate contracts have been the source of litigation and costly court battles.

9. AVOID: Buying a home where contingency clauses are not used to provide for uncertainties. For example, if you want the purchase to be contingent upon your ability to qualify for new financing, language to this effect should be incorporated into the contract.

10. AVOID: Buying a home where the lender has a due-on-sales clause that allows more than a 2 percent increase in the interest rate.

11. AVOID: Purchasing a home without first having a home inspection conducted by a competent housing inspector or someone else who is knowledgeable about home construction.

12. AVOID: Buying a home using a large down payment to reduce the mortgage payment unless the purpose is to reduce the term of the loan. The buyer could in most cases save more money by investing in mutual funds, certificates of deposits, and treasury bills. Liquidity is maintained with these investments. Funds are locked into the home when large down payments are used.

13. AVOID: Purchasing a home without first examining the various methods of financing. The financing method chosen should be based upon the buyer's financial structure and conditions and not upon the feasibility in procuring the loan.

14. AVOID: Overbuying where the home's functional use is much greater than or incompatible with the homebuyer's needs.

15. AVOID: Purchasing a home in a neighborhood where there

is a high incidence of crime, including vandalisim. These two conditions adversely affect property values and make the home difficult to sell.

16. AVOID: Purchasing homes in neighborhoods where home maintenance is neglected. This condition is highly visible and can be detected easily by the buyer. Neighborhoods where a preponderance of the homes are poorly maintained should be avoided, regardless of the amenities that the home has. Even with all the amenities, the home would be difficult to resell.

17. AVOID: Purchasing homes adjacent to industrial areas where, because of their operations, noise and air pollution have become a neighborhood nuisance.

18. AVOID: Buying a home that has been overbuilt for the neighborhood where it is located. These homes become white elephants and are difficult to resell. Regardless of the amenities, the home is nonconforming and may have minimal appreciation.

19. AVOID: Buying a home where the selling price exceeds the market value. The net appreciation in market price may be offset by the excessive selling price. Equity accumulation grows at a below-average rate.

20. AVOID: Buying a home that has inadequate home insurance. In case of damage by natural causes or accidents, there may not be enough coverage to completely repair the house.

21. AVOID: Purchasing a home in a neighborhood that does not have ready access to major and essential services. Modern shopping facilities and medical and recreational facilities increase the market value of homes. These services also increase the marketability of the home.

22. AVOID: Purchasing a home in a neighborhood where the time of turnover exceeds nine months. The ideal neighborhood would be where homes are sold within six months from the date they are listed.

23. AVOID: Purchasing a home from a seller who refuses to negotiate interest at a rate that is below market rate on owner's carrybacks.

24. AVOID: Buying a home from a seller who insists that the buyer pays the points and the closing costs. The owner should pay for the points. Closing costs are generally divided among the buyer and the seller.

25. AVOID: Purchasing a home from a seller where the sale is contingent upon the seller purchasing another home. Unless there is a consideration, the buyer may be prevented from buying another home where the terms are more advantageous.

Housing Glossary

ACCELERATION CLAUSE. A clause that is used in a note or mortgage and allows the creditor to foreclose on the property in the event the debtor defaults on the note or causes economic waste that reduces the market value of the property.

AD VALOREM TAXES. Taxes imposed on the property that are based on the assessed value.

ADJUSTED RATE MORTGAGE (ARM). The interest that is adjusted on the basis of an index. The amount applied to the principal balance may increase or decrease.

AMORTIZATION. The process where equal loan payments are paid over a specified period of time to pay off the loan.

APPRAISAL. A determination made by an appraiser of the market value of the property at a specific time.

ASSESSED VALUATION. The value that is placed on the property by local governments to determine the amount of real estate tax that must be paid. There is a substantial difference between the market value and the assessed value of the property. The market value normally is considerably less than the assessed value.

ASSESSMENT. A fee that the property incurs as a result of improvements such as streets, sewers, sidewalks, or lights.

ASSIGNMENT OF MORTGAGE. An instrument that is used to transfer a mortgage from one mortgagee to another one.

ASSUMPTION OF MORTGAGE. A condition under which a buyer purchases property by agreeing to pay the existing mortgage payment. The written consent of the mortgagee is required to release the original mortgagor from financial responsibility.

BALLOON MORTGAGE. A financial plan where interest-only payments are paid, with the full amount of the principal balance due at the end of the term.

BROKER. A person who is employed to bring the buyer and seller together for the purpose of consummating a contract to exchange title to property for agreed financial terms.

BUY INTEREST DOWN MORTGAGE (BIM). A mortgage in which the interest is bought down below market value.

CERTIFICATE OF TITLE. A document issued by a title company assuring that the title is marketable and insurable. This document does not guarantee against concealed defects.

CLOSING COSTS. The expenditures incurred by both the buyer and seller in consummating real estate transactions. Certain costs are prorated and paid by both buyer and seller.

CONDOMINIUM. A multiunit housing complex where each dwelling is owned individually. A homeowners association represented by a board made up of owners develops operating policies. Each owner has access to common areas.

CONVENTIONAL MORTGAGE. A mortgage made by the lender that is not insured by HUD or the Veterans Administration. Terms and conditions vary from lender to lender.

COOPERATIVE HOUSING. An apartment that is owned by a corporation in which the stockholders are the owners of individual units. The corporation has an elected board of directors that supervises the operations of the apartments.

CREDIT RATING. A history of a person's paying habits that describes the consistency which financial obligations are paid.

DEBT-INCOME RATIO. A percentage of a person's income that is used to pay monthly debts. The higher the percentage of the income that is applied to reduce or pay debts, the less disposable income is available.

DEED OF TRUST. A document substituted for a mortgage. It is a security instrument where real property is pledged for the debt on the property.

DEFAULT. Failure on the part of the buyer to make mortgage payments according to the terms of the mortgage or trust note.

DOWN PAYMENT. The total amount of money that is paid by the buyer upon signing the sales agreement. The difference between the amount financed and the sales price is the down payment. The down payment is normally not refundable if the buyer fails to purchase the property without good cause. Conditions would be specified under which the down payment is returned by the seller.

DUE-ON-SALE CLAUSE. A clause put into a note that allows the lender to call the loan upon sale of the property.

EARNEST MONEY. A deposit of money to show that the buyer is serious and acting in good faith in buying the property. It may be returned under specific conditions.

EASEMENT RIGHTS. Rights that a person or company has to cross over property owned by another owner.

ECONOMIC WASTE. Willful neglect, abuse, misuse, and/or damage to the property caused by the person in possession.

ENCUMBERANCE. Legal interest that a person has in property owned by another. Encumbrances affect the market and decrease the value of the property. They come in different forms—liens, restrictive convenants, zoning laws, taxes, and easements.

EQUITY. The difference between the market value of the property and the outstanding existing mortgage.

ESCROW. May appear in several forms: (1) initial escrow, sales transations, and (2) post escrow, monthly mortgage payments. In the initial escrow, funds are deposited with a third party until specific contractual obligations are met. In the sale of property, the escrow agent disperses the funds to the seller. In post escrow, the buyer pays into an escrow account each month money to cover taxes, assessments, hazard insurance, and mortgage insurance premiums.

FORECLOSURE. The process whereby actions are taken to dispossess the owner who defaults or fails to comply with terms of the mortgage or deed of trust.

GRADUATED PAYMENT MORTGAGE (GPM). A HUD-insured mortgage in which the mortgage payments increase from 2 to 7½ percent for a specified number of years. The borrower actually borrows money to subsidize the mortgage loan.

GRANTEE. The party who is the buyer or receives title to property.

GRANTOR. The seller or the party who gives title to another.

GRIP. A financing instrument where interest is increased based on a floating index.

GROWING EQUITY MORTGAGE (GEM). A financing instrument in which the buyer pays greater monthly payments in order to reduce the principal, thereby paying the loan off in a shorter period of time.

HAZARD INSURANCE. A form of insurance that protects the property from fire, certain weather conditions, and other common hazards.

HOME LOAN UNDERWRITING STANDARDS. Conditions the buyer must meet to qualify for a loan to finance the property. The buyer must have employment stability, adequate income, and a good credit rating.

JOINT TENANTS. Title taken by mortgagors with rights of survivorship. Upon death of one co-mortgagor title passes to the surviving co-mortgagor.

JUDICIARY FORECLOSURE. Legal action pursued in the court in order to foreclose on an owner who has defaulted on a mortgage loan. A lender has to use the court to foreclose on an owner who used a mortgage to finance the home.

LAND SALES CONTRACT. A contractual arrangement used by a buyer to purchase a home. The title is retained by the seller until a percentage of the loan is paid or the loan is paid in full.

LEASE-OPTION PURCHASE. An arrangement made between a seller and a buyer to lease or rent a home for a specified term. Part of the rent is allocated to pay the down payment. If the buyer neglects to utilize the option to purchase, the money appropriated for the down payment may be retained by the seller.

LOAN TO VALUE. The amount of money that lender will loan the borrower on property that is pledged as security for the loan. The total amount of money loaned is determined by taking a percentage of the equity, which is the difference between the property's market value and the outstanding mortgage balance.

MECHANICS LIEN. A lien that is placed against property by a contractor or supplier for work done on the property or materials used to improve or make repairs on the property.

MORTGAGE. A legal instrument by which the borrower pledges a security for money loaned to finance the property.

MORTGAGE INSURANCE PREMIUM. A monthly charge that is made by the homeowner to the lender on behalf of HUD. This money is used as a form of insurance to protect lenders and reduce the cost of HUD's insurance program.

MORTGAGE PAYMENT SHOCK AFFECT. A condition where the mortgage payments substantially increase during the adjusted period, affecting the homebuyer's ability to maintain the mortgage in a current state. This condition usually occurs when a home is purchased with a substantial interest discount the first year and large subsequent mortgage payment increases.

MORTGAGEE. The lender who provides the funds to purchase the property.

MORTGAGOR. The person borrowing the money to finance the purchase of the property.

NEGATIVE AMORTIZATION. A condition that occurs when the index changes so existing payment does not cover the amount of the monthly accrued interest. The difference between the payment and the accrued interest is added to the principal balance of the loan.

NONJUDICIARY FORECLOSURE. A proceeding used by the lender to foreclose on a homebuyer who defaulted on a trust note. Court action is not necessary in order to foreclose. The lender can avoid expensive legal actions and substantially reduce the length of foreclosure time. Nonjudiciary foreclosures are generally involved when a person purchases a home using a trust note.

NOVATION. The substitution of a new legal obligation for an old one. In real estate terms, the buyer assumes the seller's legal obligation to repay the financial obligation of the loan.

PITI. Principal, Interest, Taxes, and Insurance represent the total payments that collected by the lender. A fixed amount of the payments is held in an escrow account to pay the taxes and hazard insurance. The remainder is applied toward the principal and interest.

POINTS. A one time fee charge by the lender as additional interest revenue. One point is 1 percent. HUD and the Veterans Administration prohibit the buyer from paying points. On conventional, the points may be paid by either the buyer or seller.

PREPAID EXPENSES. Money that is deposited to cover hazard insurance, taxes, mortgage insurance premimums, and interest.

PREPAYMENT PENALTY. A fee charge by the lender for paying off the loan before the due date. FHA-insured Loans do not contain the penalty clause.

PRINCIPAL. That amount that is owed on the property. Part of the monthly payments is used to reduce the outstanding balance, with a specific percentage paid as interest.

PURCHASE MONEY MORTGAGE. A mortgage that the buyer gives to the seller as part of the purchase price of the property.

QUIT CLAIM DEED. A deed used to transfer the interest that one has in the property.

REAL ESTATE PROCEDURES ACT (RESPA). A federal law that is designed to control costs incurred in real estate transactions. The law requires the lender to give the buyer a "good faith estimate" of the closing costs within three days after the buyer submits a loan application.

RECLINING. Areas in which lenders deny mortgage loans.

REDLINING. The practice used by lenders to restrict home loans to residents owning property in certain areas.

REINSTATEMENT OF MORTGAGE. A schedule of mortgage payments designed to bring a delinquent mortgage current.

RENEGOTIABLE MORTGAGE. A mortgage that is renegotiated at specified intervals to reflect the change in interest rate. This feature is also used in other mortgages.

RESERVE ACCOUNT MORTGAGE (RAM). An instrument that is used to allow another party to put up money for the buyer without becoming a party to the transaction. The money is held in a special interest bearing account. It is returned to the donor within a specified time or when certain conditions occur.

RESPA. Real Estate Settlement Procedures Act. Closing costs estimates that the lender is required to send the borrower within three business days. Lenders are also limited to the amount of money that can be held in the escrow account for property taxes and insurance.

RESTRICTIVE CONVENANTS. Certain conditions that are put in deeds to restruct the use of property. Example: conditions that place limitations on style and price of homes that can be built or how property can be used by the buyer.

REVERSE ANNUITY MORTGAGE. A mortgage designed for elderly homeowners. The equity that has been accumulated is converted to a monthly annuity that is based upon the amount of annuity in the home and the expected life of the homeowner.

185

REVERSION. Provisions that allows the former owner of property to repossess it if the buyer fails to comply with contractual terms.

RIGHT OF RECISSION. A provision in the truth-in-lending law that allows the borrower to cancel a contract within three days after it has been signed. If the property is encumbered by a lien against the property, the provision is enforceable.

SALES LEASEBACK. An arrangement where the homeowners sell their home to an investor and enter into a rental agreement to lease it back from the investor. This arrangement is especially beneficial to elderly homeowners who wish to capitalize on the equity in their homes.

SATISFACTION OF MORTGAGE. A document given to the borrower to show evidence that the debt on the property has been paid.

SECOND MORTGAGE. A mortgage that is given to a person or company that is secondary to the first. In the event of foreclosure, proceeds from the sale goes first to pay the first mortgage. The remaining proceeds, if any, are applied to the second mortgage.

SHARED APPRECIATION MORTGAGE. An instrument that allows a party to act as co-mortgagor for the purpose of sharing in the appreciated value of the property.

SPECIAL ASSESSMENT. A fee imposed on property for making special improvements such as streets, sewer, sidewalks, or streetlights.

SUBORDINATION CLAUSE. A clause used in a note or mortgage that acknowledges a prior lien that has first claim in case the property is liquidated for nonpayment of the debt against the property.

TENANTS IN COMMON. Join ownership by two or more persons without rights of survivorship.

TITLE. The interest a person has in property. The legal instrument to show ownership and/or possession is in the form of a deed.

TITLE INSURANCE. Insurance that protects the owner and lender against the loss resulting from title defects.

TRUST DEED. A security instrument that is used to replace a mortgage. Under a trust deed, title is conveyed to a third party (trustee), to be held until the debt is paid in full.

TRUSTEE. An agency or person who has the legal responsibility of holding title to property for the beneficiary until performances specified in the trust note are satisfied.

UNREASONABLE RESTRAINT ON ALIENATION. Condition that exists when a lender enforces the due-on-sale provision. It affects the marketability of the property, causing the buyer to change his mind because the lender increases the interest rate, thereby restraining the seller in selling the property.

WRAPAROUND MORTGAGE. A technique used to blend the interest rate on an existing mortgage with the current interest rate on a new second mortgage with an interest rate that is lower than the market rate.

Index

Outside maintenance, 58
Outstanding collection accounts, 116
Over and under buying, 7
Overall financial control plans, 43
Overheated economy, 90
Overspending, 79
Overzealous buyer, 8
Owner carryback arrangement, 124, 125

Pattern of consistment payment, 51
Partial payment, 65
Penalty provision, 30
PITI, 85
Pledge account mortgage, 166, 167
Plumbing, 28
Poor credit rating, 49
Power through bylaws, 60
Predominantly minority ownership, 38
Principal mortgage balance, 109
Private mortgage insurance corportions, 104
Probate courts, 22
Professional housing inspector, 28
Projected income, 92
Principal residence, 70, 71
Prospective condominium buyers, 62
Prevailing interest rates, 129, 130

Qualify for a specific amount, 19
Quality and availability of shopping center, 19
Quality of schools, 5

Racial discrimination, 36
Racial steering, 37
RAM, 121
Recapture percentage, 164
Recertification computation, 164
Recurring bills, 11
Reduction in income, 72
Reestablishing credit reliability, 52
Regional index, 84
Remainder right, 123
Renegotiable mortgage, 128, 129
Rental income, 70
Repaired market value, 83
Repayment plan, 51
Repressive financial restraints, 45
Resale of home, 20
Reserve account mortgage, 131, 132
Residual income, 148
RESPA, 34
Reverse Annuity Mortgage, 121
Right of Survivorship, 23
Right of Redemption, 40
Rigid debt control system, 45

Rollover mortgage, 129

Sales leaseback plan, 122, 123
Sales of residential property, 76
Section 234, 68
Section 804E, 37
Second mortgage, 140, 141
Selecting a neighborhood, 4
Security instrument, 98
Selecting an ARM, 89
Selection criteria, 3
Seller's loan number, 102
Selling price, 115
Severely distressed sellers, 56
Shared appreciation mortgage, 134, 135
Sharing load bearing walls, 6
Single deed condominium estates, 60
Slow credit, 51
Specific income bracket, 154
Specific performances, 33
Specified percentage of option money, 116
Split equity arrangement, 123
Standard fixed rate mortgage, 87
Structural condition, 29
Subsidized rental housing, 122
Substantial equity, 104
Submitting a bid to purchase a home, 83
Substantial interest in the home, 75
Substantial reduction in income, 152
Substantial rehabilitation, 159
Surviving co-mortgagor, 134

Temporary employment, 47
Temporary equity, 131
Tenancy by the entirety, 23
Title company, 33, 119
Title VII, 36
Total housing expense, 12, 13
Traditional financing methods, 120
Traditional mortgages, 165
Trustee, 39
Trustor, 39
Treasury notes, 84
Turnover rate, 76

Unaffordable dream home, 102
Uncovering electrical defects, 28
Uncovering defects, 169
Undesirable elements that affect market values, 18
Underwriting standards, 85, 148
Unforseen variables, 113
Uninsured damage, 71
Unpaid monthly association fees, 60
Undivided interest in common estates, 61
Unplanned purchases, 80